Ulrich Kellerer

One Moment Can Change Your Life!

Extraordinary Stories about Ordinary People

Foreword by Jack Canfield,
Author of the bestselling "Chicken Soup for the Soul"® series,
"The Success Principles" and "Tapping into Success"

*I dedicate this book
to my twin brother Thomas
who was born
twenty minutes before me.*

*His entire life changed
completely within an instant.*

*May he and my brother Ralf,
along with my mother and father,
be open to new dimensions
until we meet again one day.*

Copyright © by Ulrich Kellerer 2018

All rights reserved.

www.ulrich-kellerer.com

Translation: Christine Louise Hohlbaum

ISBN-13: 978-1986551229

ISBN-10: 1986551229

Table of Contents

Foreword 9
Introduction 12
The Final Leap 20
An Unforgettable Night in the Mountains 28
You May Be Poor, but Don't Ever Be Pathetic! 34
There is Good in Everything 38
The Happiest Moment in My Marriage 50
An Unusual Encounter 60
Four Best Friends 64
A Life-Changing Decision 76
It was the Year 1954 84
Like Phoenix From the Ashes 86
Never Lose Yourself 100
An Unbelievable Discovery 104
There is Only One Father 106
A New Horizon 114
Emergency Call from the Heart 122
Train of Thought: From Constriction to Vastness 128
My American Dream 132
I was "the loser" 136
An Experience That Turned Everything on its Head 142
Never Say Never... 148
Barbara's Healing Story 154
How One Decision Changes Everything 160
It´s My Life! 164
Our Engine Stopped! 168
My Second Life 174
What chance would we have missed! 178
Epilogue 184
Acknowledgments 194

Foreword

by Jack Canfield

Author of the megaselling Chicken Soup for the Soul® series, The Success Principles and Tapping into Success

I have spent nearly my entire life researching and writing about what makes the most successful people so successful. What sets them apart from the others? Are they smarter, faster, more rational, more organized, more creative, more talented – or are they simply the lucky ones upon whom fate has smiled so kindly?

And then there is the question of exactly what is success? The truth is success means different things to different people. Unfortunately, most people tend to only think of success in terms of business, professional and financial success.

One of the things I have learned in studying successful people is that successful people deal with change better than other people. They embrace change and they roll with it. They have learned that change is inevitable. As one pundit once observed, "The only thing that never changes is change." We see it in the changing seasons, in how are bodies inevitably change, the never-ending and rapid change in technology, regime changes, and in our intimate and family relationships. No matter how hard we may want to hold on to the way it is or the way it was, change keeps occurring. Resisting it is futile.

Sometimes change comes slowly and is predictable, and sometimes it comes suddenly and unexpectedly. Sudden unexpected changes like losing your job, the death of a loved one, divorce, new competitors for your business, the loss of a major account, an economic crash, a catastrophic illness or accident can be life altering in ways we wish wouldn't happen, but when we embrace them and roll with them, we see that they are inviting us to call forth and integrate new parts of ourselves like creativity, resilience, patience, courage, compassion and unconditional love. As Napoleon Hill so brilliantly taught us, "Every negative event contains within it the seed of an equal or greater benefit." But we have to look for it. Wallowing in self-pity, blaming and complaining will not yield the new insights, wisdom and personal development that is potentially contained in every seemingly negative change.

On the other hand, unexpected events can create positive life changes. Falling in love, sudden fame, receiving unexpected invitations, gifts and inheritances, and sudden epiphanies can change your life. But even these seemingly positive events can have challenges. What if you are already married? What if you don't want the responsibility of stewarding a large amount of money or afraid all your friends will now see you as a source of loans.

Several years ago I met Ulrich Kellerer at a seminar in Philadelphia. From the get-go he impressed me with his kindness, seriousness and openness as he told me about his life. And what a life he's led! He is not only the successful entrepreneur of an international fashion label, he is also a compassionate son and a devoted husband as well as a social activist.

"Ulrich the German," as some of us respectfully and jokingly called him during the seminar, earned my deepest respect as he shared his ideas, insights and his vision to make a significant difference in the life of others. As a result I highly encouraged him to put his thoughts and experiences into book form in order to inspire others.

I am very proud that Ulrich trusted me enough to follow my advice, and that the result is this book – *One Moment Can Change Your Life!*

This book, if you really allow it to penetrate you as you read it, can change your life. Ulrich has gathered, compiled and mindfully commented on the incredible stories of everyday people. It is a treasure trove of inspiration, and as some early readers have commented, "It is almost like literary therapy."

The book is about people whose lives changed in the blink of an eye. For the most part, the book centers around the attitudes the people had as they experienced dramatic change – sometimes they accepted it with all their heart, sometimes with great joy, sometimes virtually against their will or with great anguish. But in every single case, the people's lives were ultimately enriched, if not dramatically improved, when they actively dealt with the change they faced.

Ulrich has selected stories that speak both to our hearts and our minds. They are stories that encourage, comfort, inspire and cause us to reflect about our own lives. Above all, they show us that we are not alone.

Jack Canfield, Spring 2017

Introduction

One Moment Can Change Your Life!
by Ulrich Kellerer

We are living in fast times. Speed seems to be the ultimate maxim. „Faster, farther, higher!" That is how we define our goals. We barely find the time or energy to take a step back and reflect where we come from and where we are headed. What is our purpose in life – in this world?

Is it really material things that make us happy? Does an individual have the potential to live a self-determined life? Haven't we all been given certain abilities to lead a life worth living? Don't we all have intuition, an inner voice and a sense of what is right and wrong?

My motivation to write this book arose from numerous conversations I have had with many people. I soon realized that every one of us has a personal story in which we have experienced a pivotal moment in our lives that changed everything.

The most important human trait is the ability to communicate. Every one of us should tell our stories to help, inspire and motivate others.

Every experience described in this book is based on a true story. They are stories about everyday people of varying ages and backgrounds. This is where my story begins:

Our home was a farm situated in the alpine uplands of Bavaria. It was a working farm that had been in our family for generations. My father was a reporter and editor for a local newspaper. My mother devoted all her time and love raising her three sons – my eldest brother and us twins. I was the youngest twin.

My father had no ambitions to take over the family farm so we finally moved to a small city in Bavaria. Our lives were harmonious and, for the first few years of my life, quite protected within the safety of my family. Until that moment in which everything changed.

At the age of four, my twin brother Thomas and I had to get an oral vaccination, which was customary for children our age back then. Tragically, what the doctors did not know at the time, was that Thomas was in an early stage of developing the measles. The result was a life-long injury that caused him to have epileptic fits and turned him into a mentally disabled person.

Thomas had to suffer through one-and-a-half years at a hospital in Munich. Our mother tried to visit him as much as possible. She would spend the entire day traveling by train or hitchhiking to do so. Thomas couldn't understand what happened and why his mommy didn't bring him home.

The doctors gave up on him, saying he would never learn to draw a circle, much less learn how to read and write.

By virtue of necessity and to support similarly affected families, my parents founded a non-profit organization called „Support for Mentally and Physically Disabled Children" in Rosenheim, Bavaria.

Unlike the doctors who didn't believe Thomas would ever improve, our mother never gave up. Thanks to her, Thomas received the assistance and support he needed. She was the one who got him to learn how to read and write. While he couldn't visit a regular school, he was able to attend a school for mentally and physically disabled children that included a sheltered workshop. There he would be able to receive school instruction and learn a trade.

My twin brother recognized very early that – with no fault of his own -- his life had been completely changed. His brothers attended a regular school, had friends and girlfriends and were able to do all the things of which he could only dream. It was very painful for him to realize that such a life was never meant to be for him.

Humans are incredibly adaptable. One can be grateful for the positive moments, too.

But I would like to tell you another story: my own. It is about something that changed my life in an instant and that still affects me to this day.

When I was sixteen years old, my father, who smoked three packs of cigarettes a day, was diagnosed with throat cancer. He underwent an operation in which the doctors removed his entire larynx. When I went to visit him shortly after the operation, my father wanted to communicate something to me. He tried to speak, but only air blew through the hole in his throat. He was incredibly angry and upset because I could not understand him. It was one of the worst moments in both of our lives.

Crying and completely beside myself, I ran down the hallway of the hospital and out the building. The next morning I lay in bed, praying to God that he should make me pay for a few of my own sins. I wanted to do something to make it better for my father by taking away part of his pain.

The next morning I got up to go school as I did every day and forgot my prayer. But on the way to school, I suddenly experienced extreme stomach pains that kept me hunched over so I couldn't even walk upright. I pretty much crawled on all fours along the street. Shortly before I reached the school building, my schoolmates called an ambulance. I thought it might be appendicitis. The ambulance brought me to the emergency room. My mother quickly came, but then we had to wait three hours for a diagnosis: a pancreatic infection!

The doctors claimed I drank too much alcohol, which my mother firmly and angrily denied. The pain was unbearable and they finally brought me to intensive care. The last thing I remember were seven doctors hovering over me. My jaw popped out of its socket, I babbled on like a baby and fell into a coma.

What happened next was the best experience of my young life. I saw colors I had never seen before; I heard music that doesn't exist on this Earth. I reached a gate where a voice asked me if I wanted to walk through it or if I wished to return to Earth.

I knew without a doubt that it must be God. An infinite feeling of joy ran through my entire body. I absolutely wanted to walk through that gate – but I was only sixteen years old! And I just had to tell my parents and my girlfriend about this extraterrestrial experience. In that moment I decided to return to life.

The doctors said it was a medical miracle when I awoke from my coma four days later. Because the pancreas is the only organ that „digests itself" when it is as infected as mine was, they had already told my mother to make funeral arrangements.

Shortly thereafter I was released from the hospital and enjoyed my new life to the fullest. Pretty soon, however, I started having dreams about accidents and people dying, all of which came true.

I would have these déjà-vu experiences shortly before the accidents would occur. I always knew that something was about to happen. Because of these premonitions and predictions, I soon became an outsider in my circle of friends. They distanced themselves from me, saying I was strange. At first in jest, their remarks became increasingly venomous as they shouted: „Don't you even think of dreaming about me!"

I couldn't handle it. I wanted to live a normal life. I wanted to be like everyone else! As a result, I suppressed and negated my unsettling abilities and stopped writing down and analyzing my dreams.

After finishing my business degree, I asked my company to move me to one of their foreign offices so that I could work there and get some distance from Germany and my own spirituality.

In France I was responsible in the company for managing the packaging production for food that was manufactured there. After I learned that they used water to dilute the food supply, I asked to speak with my German employer. They assured me that it was completely legal and that France had different laws. I earned a lot of money, received bonuses and even had an apartment the company paid for...

But somehow I couldn't reconcile it all with my own conscience. So I quit and for the first time in my life, I was unemployed. In a single weekend, I moved out of the apartment in France and was released from my position in the company.

I started to apply for jobs. The world of fashion had always fascinated me so I pursued a position in the fashion industry.

Shortly thereafter, a friend of mine told me that the head of „Marc O'Polo" was looking for sales representatives in the individual territories in Germany as he wanted to start a second clothing line with Italian jeans. So I applied for the territory in Bavaria – and got the job.

Financially, it was a step back for me. Because I had zero experience in the textile industry, I had to start at the bottom rung of the career ladder. I spent the first three months during my probationary period in the warehouse. My boss quickly recognized that I was his best warehouse worker so he gave me the opportunity to travel throughout Bavaria with one of his veteran sales reps to introduce me to his clients as the new field rep for the Italian jeans brand „Mason's".

In record time I became a very successful field rep; my income and commissions skyrocketed from month to month. Great clothing, a company car, business trips, trade shows in foreign cities, interacting with beautiful women – I was enamored by my new life.

It was a dream come true and so very different from the hard work I had done before. This superficial world held me tight in its grip and I enjoyed going to parties, clubs, meeting women and drinking. It all seemed so perfect. Nothing could stand in the way of having a career in the fashion industry.

The inner voice that always guided me to help me decide what was right or wrong and held me accountable for what I did seemed to be a million miles away. It was a voice I would ignore for years.

Before we go down that path, let's first turn to those stories of people who had to experience the single moment in time that altered their entire existence.

The Final Leap
von Stefan F.

„Believe me. I really did want to jump!" I told Margarete. With that her ears perked as she listened to my unbelievable life story.

„But you are such a happy, joyful man! I simply can't imagine it," she replied, this petite, elderly lady who sat to my left.

I just happened to enter a conversation with her during my train ride from Munich to Berlin. Because we shared the same compartment and she appeared to be very chatty, it was easy to start a conversation with this very lovely, carefully coiffed and elegantly dressed lady.

You know the type of person that you suddenly find yourself telling your entire life story to, as I was doing in that moment. I have the tendency to keep things to myself, but her maternal vibe was the key to opening myself up in that way.

"Thanks for the compliment. That's very kind of you. But believe me I really wanted to do it. In the end it was a huge turning point in my life." Ms. Margarete Sch. – the full name of my compartment companion – wanted to respond right away; but she held herself back in the most polite and ladylike manner by simply placing a hand over her mouth.

But let's start from the beginning.

It was December 24, Christmas Eve and five days after my thirty-sixth birthday. It was a terrible day. Not only did the bad weather with its snow showers, frigid temperatures and fog of depression hang over me. I was also at the end of my rope emotionally. I felt miserable. Like a looser. Most people I know aren't familiar with my dark side that ruptured my crusty skin on that day like a volcano whose blistering lava threatened to catapult my entire being into a rotting downward spiral of emotions.

But yes. I had days like these. I would ignore the signs that seemed to roll over my like a freight train and completely darken my mood. I hadn't wanted to create the precarious situation I was in at the time; but somehow I always seemed to provoke it.

On this particular day it seemed even more intense than usual. One of my more serious relationships had failed – again – and a family had been torn apart as a result. Yet another one of my children was confronted with a painful separation that I had desperately tried to prevent. I somehow saw it coming and wanted to turn things around. But I didn't know how.

I wanted to steer things in a different direction, but I found myself without a compass and no light in the fog of others' advice.

As a result, I felt clueless. In the end my ship capsized in its own harbor that I had always thought to be so safe.

That same fog enshrouded me on this so-called happy Christmas holiday. It was 7 p.m. The moon had assumed its stately position in the night sky and cast a little light, along with the handful of street lamps, into my car window. The temperature outside had dropped to the freezing point in the last few hours. I had been in the office up to that point to distract myself and think about other things. As if it were that easy! Especially at that time of year when you are constantly confronted with images of happy families all around you. If you even have one. Not to mention one that loves you in a happy home.

I had none of those things anymore. I was practically homeless, penniless and without a family. After my separation, I moved into a small cabin owned by some friends. They kindly offered it to me because I couldn't find anything else on such short notice. Financially, I had been at my limit for the past few months.

My income covered child support, but it no longer allowed for me to live a normal life. Yes, I had children. But they did not live with me. They stayed with their mothers and grandparents – with their own families, in other words. And in case you stumbled over the word "mothers," yes: There were two. Two mothers, one child each, one failed relationship each. I was the only common denominator in the whole damn thing. This fact made me doubt my ability to ever have a successful relationship and family life.

During the winter my cabin was always freezing because the heat did not work well. On this particular day I didn't want to bother anyone by asking for help. Instead I got in my car and drove. Blasting the heat in the car and turning up the temperature gauge that regulated the heated seats, I drove to my office for a few hours, then cruised aimlessly around the area. I turned off the radio because I couldn't bear the sound of Christmas music.

As a child of divorce, I had my own difficult history with family life. Unfortunately, I allowed myself to get between my parents and to get pulled into their drama. I constantly felt guilty and ashamed. A few months prior I even cut off all contact with my mother out of self-protection because I no longer knew who she really was.

Caught up in her own problems, she constantly tried to manipulate me, using subtle accusations to move me in the direction she wanted me to be. For the longest time I didn't notice what she was doing. I remained silent. Now it was too late to rescue my own family life as her manipulations had spread through my current relationship like poison. There was no way out.

I had an ambiguous relationship with my father. When he visited, it was always very nice, but unfortunately he was more interested in advancing his career than spending time with me. Today, on Christmas Eve, he spent the day with his parents-in-law, the parents of his new wife. As in years past, I once again showed my understanding, but declined their invitation to join them in their Christmas festivities. A small part of me had hoped he would decide to spend that time with me alone. But he did not and I was once again left by myself.

Then there was my brother. My connection with him had weakened ever since I had decided to be who I am and live my own life and no longer try to satisfy his expectations of who I should be. You might see it as an excuse for my lack of action, which it was in part, but sometimes you need to fall on your face a time or two before you start to see things more clearly. Especially when it comes to your own family members, whom you hope to see act selflessly at least once in their lives.

In short, everything came to a head that day. My situation couldn't have been worse. I felt alone, like a failure and unlovable. I stopped at the bridge crossing the Inn River and parked my car in a side street. After a few moments of silence, the most profound feelings of grief overcame me as the tears began to fall down my cheeks.

It was over. I didn't want to hang on any longer. I couldn't. To be completely alone and to feel responsible for simply everything was too much for me to handle. I couldn't take it anymore.

The rain had turned to a soft snowfall as I slowly opened the car door. I got out of the car and moved toward the bridge. At this point I felt as if I had been drugged. I could no longer take in anything that was happening around me. It was totally quiet. No cars were on the street. My vision narrowed to a singular goal. When I reached the middle of the bridge, I lifted myself up onto the bridge railing with the help of a lamppost. At the same time I looked down at the surging water. The river current, along with the weight of my clothing, would assure everything would be over quickly.

I was determined to put an end to my misery. I closed my eyes, which made me feel unsteady. Once again all the negative thoughts came rushing into my mind that had convinced me to take the final step and end it all. A slight wind at my back pushed me in the right direction. Just as my fingers started to release their grip on the lamppost, I heard someone off in the distance calling me. There were actually two tender voices that kept saying the same thing over and over again: "Dearest Daddy! We need you because we love you so much. Please don't leave us alone!"

At first I couldn't really decipher the words, but as I heard them a second and a third time, they hit me like a ton of bricks. My legs weakened and I collapsed, falling toward the bridge railing and backwards onto the sidewalk. One hand was still on the bridge railing as I pulled myself up and began to cry wretchedly, harder than I had ever cried in my entire life.

But this time I cried out of anger toward my own behavior. What kind of selfish asshole was I? How could I have been so blind? God knows I was no better than the people I judged. Out of desperation for my near-suicide, I remained crouched on the spot for a few minutes until I finally got up and moved back toward the car. It was the call of my children, that expression of unconditional love, that had changed my life forevermore. It was a wake-up call out of the coma of self-pity about my past.

"I am so glad you made it." Those were Margarete´s whispered parting words before she got off the train. She was right. I was glad that I did not jump that day. I now know that all the pain that life or family members in our younger years offer can be overcome.

And even though it was a long, hard road to get to the light that I refused to see for the longest time, I now know that I am worthy of love. And that was the final leap for me – the leap toward my own freedom.

An Unforgettable Night in the Mountains

by Karen P.

It was March and as with every year, we had planned a weekend of skiing with friends in the mountains. Over the years we had grown to a group of twenty people consisting of women and men from a wide range of backgrounds.

We enjoyed the best weather on our way to the mountains even though the weather forecast didn't sound too good. When we arrived to the ski resort, we enjoyed a wonderful day of skiing with our friends. In the evening we made plans to go sledding down the hill as we did every year.

I remember the hotel owner warning us not to go to the sledding hill because a thin sheet of ice had formed on top of the snow. But we were not to be stopped. I was less motivated to go sledding than I was to go skiing. But since everyone was so excited to go – especially my husband – I caved and agreed to join them.

They pulled us up to the cabin with a tractor and wagon. The atmosphere in the mountains at night was amazing. We sat together and had a great time. My best friend had joined us with her ten-year-old son for the first time. Night sledding was an absolute highlight for him. He could hardly wait until he could start down the slope.

My husband wanted to set off right after dinner. So the four of us – my husband, my best friend, her son and I – took off as the advanced sledding party down the mountain.

It had already grown dark outside. Our sleds already stood at the ready in front of the cabin. At the head of the pack was my husband, of course. He was in the best of moods and filled with anticipation. Behind him were my best friend and her son, followed by myself as the caboose. Each of us had a flashlight to illuminate the way. Because I am a bit of a scaredy-cat when it comes to sledding, I was happy to be the last in the group of four because I could go at my own pace.

As a result, I soon found myself all alone on the path. I couldn't see the lights of my sledding companions. Slowly and at a snail's pace, I attempted to reach the valley safely along the icy path.

About halfway down, I suddenly stopped in the middle of the forest. To this day I have no idea why. It was as if my inner voice had stopped me. Despite the icy ground I got off my sled and looked around. Crazy, right? To stop in the middle of the forest in the complete dark where no one could be found for miles and miles and look around.

To the left of me, I could see an abyss. My breath stagnated as I turned off my flashlight. Something had happened! Pulling the sled behind me on shaky legs, I felt my way to the abyss and illuminated the area with my flashlight. My blood ran cold at the sight I saw.

My husband was hanging with his face up between two rocks. A small branch had punctured his eyebrow. Step by step I fought my way to him. He was slightly out of it and not quite responsive. In a knee-jerk response, I removed the branch from his eyebrow and tried to lie him down on the ground. The back of his head was bleeding profusely and he had a huge cut behind his ear.

In this dire situation, which felt more like a movie than real life, I tried to call the mountain rescue team, but I couldn't remember the number. I was desperate! Then I tried to call my best friend who must have reached the end of the slope by now. Luckily I had reception and could explain the situation to her.

She rushed back to us, walking with her son along the icy slope to the scene of the accident. Because I did not know exactly where we were, I made signals with my flashlight. After what felt like hours, they finally reached us and saw what had happened. We decided her son should stay with me and my injured husband while she notified the rescue team and told them where we were.

My friend's son and I stayed at the scene of the accident for about one and one-half hours. During that time we tried to help my husband the best we could, pushing our sleds together and placing him on them. We took care of the wound on his head with tissues and snow. He kept wanting to fall asleep, but we talked to him continuously to keep him awake so that his body didn't cool down too much.

I notified our friends at the cabin via cell phone. At first they thought it was a joke until they realized the seriousness of the accident. They immediately came down the slope with their sleds. I warned them about the danger of the ice and that they should be very careful. Besides, a few of our friends with us had never been on a sled before.

When they reached the scene of the accident, they were completely shocked. Luckily, one of the members of our group was a doctor who immediately took care of him. I had instinctively done the right things by placing him on his side and applying pressure to stop the bleeding.

Shortly thereafter an emergency doctor arrived in a Jeep. Because the slope was so narrow, he had to drive all the way up the mountain to turn around. We placed my husband on a gurney and drove to the hospital. The doctor diagnosed him with multiple muscle tears in his shoulder. They stapled the wounds on his head and eyebrow.

Because the hospital was overcrowded, the doctor told me my husband couldn't stay. I was instructed to take him to a hotel and come back the next day or drive home and take him to the local hospital there. Possibly his skull had sustained hairline factures, but they wouldn't be able to determine that until the next day after a more thorough examination. They gave me some pills for him to tide himself over during the night. They told me to observe him very closely for the next hours in case his condition worsened or froth started to spill out of his mouth. In that event I should come back right away.

I will never forget that night for as long as I live. For the first time in our long and wonderful relationship, I realized how quickly you could lose someone you love. We had been just a few meters apart from one another and this accident could have had unthinkable consequences.

To this day I am so grateful for my inner voice that moved me to stop at that exact spot and get off the sled. If I had been just a few meters before or after the scene of the accident, I may not have seen my husband. Further it was very fortunate that his flashlight lay in the exact position it did so that I could even see its light.

My husband recovered from his wounds very well and luckily he sustained no permanent damage. We no longer go sledding. No problem for me – and my husband? Well, he's decided not to tempt fate either.

A very good friend of ours once told my husband that every person has a guardian angel. Lucky for him that he knows his – and even knows what she looks like …

You May Be Poor, but Don't Ever Be Pathetic!

by Helene von Q.

It is amazing how just a few defining moments can form your character for life.

My father, who had fought during the Russian Revolution in 1917, was forced to flee at that time. First to Austria, then to Germany. He settled in Munich where he later met his wife – my mother – at a German-Russian club. After World War II, as the cities in Germany had been bombed and burned to the ground, fleeing was a real odyssey for most people. I went from Munich to the little town of Lenggries and then to Augsburg.

I found my first job in a museum in the local housing complex called "Fuggerei", a walled medieval enclave inside the city of Augsburg. The accompanying apartment was sold and torn down a few years later, forcing me to move once again.

My father was very wise about life: "Don't get attached to material things!" – "You may be poor, but don't ever be pathetic!"

His own story was quite amazing. He was a freedom fighter and worked toward the Ukraine's independence from Russia. His enormous family inheritance worth millions was destroyed during the Russian Revolution in a matter of days.

When I was little, he patiently listened to my problems until they shrank to the size of a pinhead. I learned from my father a "nobleness of heart", as we used to call it – and about what is truly important in life.

As a young girl, I studied classical dance to the point that I became a prima ballerina. But all that applause and those standing ovations after my performances didn't mean much to me. After all I had been through in my young life, I yearned more for security than fame. To give my life a solid basis, I became a seamstress and even earned my master craftsman's diploma. It was a further turning point in my life – the moment in which my career path and my existence were secured.

Through the chaos of war and the ensuing escape I was stateless and without a passport. For that reason, I could never leave Germany, not even for a brief visit to Austria, which was also responsible for the premature failure of a great love relationship that had started to develop.

My greatest life lessons were: freedom and self-discipline in all areas of life despite the highs and lows my life had to offer. The time during our escape taught me in particular not to get attached to material things. Instead, it is important to see life in a positive light and to enjoy the moment. It is not what we have, but rather who we are. And, more importantly, who *we will become!*

There is Good in Everything
by Frank C.

I was a young altar server when I tried alcohol for the first time. One time we boys tried the Communion wine after mass; another time we had a strong punch at our piano teacher's Christmas party that she kindly served us. I was ten years old.

As of about twelve years old I came into regular contact with alcohol. My father often took me to his regular evenings at the local bar where I got to try my first wheat beer. This drink seemed to fit me to a tee, especially its effects! I was suddenly "accepted" by a group of adults and that was great for my sense of self-confidence.

I liked going to the bar with my dad when he met with his group of regulars, and I started going at least once a week. I would go home after two or three beers, but I never really got drunk. Instead of church, a visit to the bar on Sundays became a regular thing.

Even after school we would meet up at a café to consume alcohol. No one gave us any trouble when we ordered alcoholic drinks as long as we were able to pay. Every once in a while we would miss the bus home…

Because alcohol – on the outside – never had any effect on me, one of my café visits at the age of thirteen ended up in alcohol poisoning. Until I left the place, I had no buzz whatsoever and that was exactly the problem. My drinking buddies fell to the ground one by one, but I only fell to my knees the moment I breathed in the fresh air outside. How I got home I'll never know. Complete blackout. It was only when I woke up in the hospital did I realize where I was. It was treated as a harmless, even great achievement to have drunk so much. I was a cool guy – at the age of thirteen!

Nonetheless I stopped drinking for a time after this incident. After a while, however, alcohol became an issue again. We would meet up after school – this time in the gym – to drink wine, vermouth and other stuff.

We would smuggle whiskey and beer into parties, but it didn't matter what the occasion was: alcohol was always a part of it. At home my friends and I were allowed to take beer from the cases in the basement. You didn't have to tell us twice and we often overdid it. We didn't meet as a group every day and we didn't get drunk every time. But we would often reach a critical point in our consumption without anyone noticing. I realized I could drink a lot more than the others. And I thought that was a great achievement!

At the age of sixteen a close friend of mine had a high-voltage accident right in front of us. In retrospect, I realize the feelings of guilt that arose from that experience were deeply connected with my friend alcohol, which was always reliable, loyal and by my side without question.

After barely graduating high school, I had no idea what to do with my life. The daily visits to the bar across from the school building during lunch that had been tolerated by idle teachers found an abrupt end.

Upon the advice of a friend I applied to the policy academy and was even accepted to the program. But I had no idea what I was getting into. I told myself I had plenty of time before my first workday. Depressed, I moved to a new city to attend the police academy there. It was very difficult to be away from home. Police work became an unmanageable task for me. It just wasn't for me because I had always stood on the other side of the law… but beer flowed there aplenty, too.

After a year I made the decision to quit. I tried my luck at applying to all kinds of administrative jobs. I really didn't know what I wanted to do, but I at least knew what I *didn't want* to do. Alcohol was always by my side in the evenings, on weekends and at every kind of party. I was able to handle so much more than the others. My tolerance level was amazing!

Finally, I applied to the German railway company. I was asked to take an acceptance test. During the initial health examination the doctor warned me even then to be careful with alcohol! But I was accepted into the program anyway at the age of nineteen. I liked working for the railway. I earned a decent income, could work independently and alcohol was available at my workplace, too. I had everything "under control," or so I thought, and the others thought so as well.

I started a serious relationship, but it failed due to my enormous alcohol consumption. I withdrew from the relationship without reason – typical for alcoholics – and even used alcohol to help me sleep. At the end of the relationship I fell into a deep hole and took my defeat at the age of twenty-two as a welcome excuse to drink even more and more often. Completely withdrawn from the world, I drank at home all alone. My condition worsened rapidly.

The physical damage through my alcohol consumption came in the form of polyneuropathy. I was sick for a long time. My house doctor discovered an alarmingly high liver count. My life literally was teetering on the precipice. I continued to lose weight, barely ate anything and only weighed 130 pounds. But I continued to sneak alcohol and told myself that no one knew about my secret drinking. I was never really drunk, maintained a certain blood alcohol level and rarely stepped out of line. Because I couldn't handle so much liquid, I moved from beer to liquor and other hard-core alcoholic drinks.

I was in such terrible condition that someone finally convinced me to seek medical attention from a neurologist and psychiatrist. I was able to open up to him and started an outpatient rehabilitation program. I was his model patient …

After a few months, I started to feel much better. The next important step was to move out of my parents' house at the age of twenty-four. I rented my own apartment and finally everything seemed to be falling into place. That fall I even took a vacation to the Canary Islands – and got a little careless. On the airplane I decided to celebrate my great mood with a little champagne and beer. Within no time I was even deeper in the mire of my own addiction. I spent the next three weeks drinking heavily: from ten o'clock in the morning, throughout the entire day and into the evening at the disco. Rum and coke until five in the morning. Then I started the whole thing over again the next day.

At home I continued the ritual, drinking myself senseless at home. If I would go out, I had to have a high blood alcohol content already to be able to appear normal in public. Every time I got behind the wheel I suffered, knowing how drunk I really was – more or less. I wasn't able to drive sober either due to the shakes, cramps and nausea I would experience. In order to get going at all, I took my first drink early in the morning. I normally couldn't keep down the first and second sips, which I would promptly vomit back up. I kept drinking until the third and fourth sips stayed down, allowing the calming warmth of the alcohol to settle into my stomach and provide me with the long-desired "clarity".

I kept trying to wean myself off alcohol on my own. I usually made it for a few days without drinking until I couldn't stand it anymore. I yearned for help and yet I denied my addiction to the outside world, something I knew in my heart of hearts was true.

During one of my many attempts at self-weaning, my body fell into an epileptic fit. I fell down the basement stairs where my parents finally found me. I had moved back in with my parents because I had started hallucinating while living by myself. I even started hearing voices. Somehow I still managed to keep my job. That year I turned twenty-eight.

I was plagued by suicidal thoughts. But I was too cowardly to actually kill myself. I really wanted to stop, but I never managed more than a few days without alcohol. It was torture without it. Family and friends withdrew from me completely. They preferred me to stay away from them. They couldn't bear to see me this way. When I remained absent, they were no longer confronted with my addiction and could relax.

Totally desperate and extremely ill, I searched for ways to change and stop drinking by replacing alcohol with pills as an alternative drug. Then I'd oscillate back to alcohol and so it went…

I was twenty-eight years old and more dead than alive.
My average was two and one-half bottles of liquor per day.

One day I received a call from a stranger. He told me he had heard from my aunt that I had an alcohol problem. He did, too. He had been sober for just a short time and knew of a great self-help group. He wanted to help me! (He was a missionary zealot as I would later become. I wanted to help everyone I could, whether they wanted my help or not.)

I was pissed! What effrontery! Who did he think he was?! Who did my aunt think she was?! I mean really … I hung up on him. But he called back a few times and finally convinced me to take down his number.

On the outside I was enraged, but deep within myself I felt something start to grow: the certainty that I wouldn't live much longer and that I had always wished to receive the help this man offered …

After drinking three bottles of wine, I built up the confidence to attend the self-help group. I was completely shocked!

These people were in an extremely good mood. They laughed and had fun, met for dinner, went out and were so lively. No aimless drunkards who would rather be dead and whom no one could understand anyway. But the people here – they knew it well because they had lived through it!

Completely thrown off track, I went home and continued to drink. I couldn't handle it! But something inside me was awakened – my need for self-preservation received nourishment.

I continued to drink. A few days later I already was rather drunk early in the morning. I didn't go to work, but called a stranger instead. I had written down his number and he had been at the self-help group too. He dropped everything, picked me up and we drove to his place. With the help of the group's director, they got me a place in a clinic and both brought me there. I resisted briefly and even wanted to jump out of the running car. I finally gave up and landed in the clinic.

I always had a certain vision, more like a paranoid vision, of how I would end up as a drunk: collapsed on the street, rushed to the hospital. Someone would give me a hospital gown with the backside open so everyone could see why I was there – everything would be out in the open!

And that is exactly what it came to. I was rushed to the hospital because of my drinking and given a hospital gown with the backside open. The only difference between my nightmare and reality was that I had been driven to the clinic. I gave up all resistance at the hospital. I stayed an entire week. Withdrawal was terrible, but I had experienced worse on my own. After a week I was released from the hospital and was allowed back to work. No one noticed at work. I had merely been ill that week …

From that point onward I visited the self-help group regularly, every week, in addition to the weekly meet-ups outside of the group. They organized private group activities as well that helped me return to a more normal life.

I never underwent clinical therapy.

After two years, I started to feel "free" and had finally become centered within myself. In these two years I lived life as I had with alcohol: I went out, visited bars and wanted to feel whether I could do it or not.

It was my way to distance myself from alcohol. It wasn't the easiest route to take and not for everyone. In retrospect it may have been easier to undergo clinical therapy. But for me it was obviously the right way to go about it.

By the age of thirty I had never felt better in my life.

I have lived without alcohol now for twenty-eight years. I still visit the self-help group. A lot of things have changed over the years, but some things still carry a lot of meaning and weight for me. People who were extremely important to me at the time are no longer with us (at least physically); new people entered my life. Everything is an ebb and flow like a river. And I am the master of my own ship.

Possible causes?
Addiction = the search for myself
Alcohol gives you a sense of belonging.
Beer is considered a staple in the Bavarian diet, which legitimizes and alleviates its consumption.
Too few people believe in themselves, have too little confidence that is compensated through alcohol.
A high tolerance level masks the real dangers of addiction.
Life-changing experiences such as the incident with my close friend unleashed feelings of guilt that I could cope with better through alcohol.
Leaving home to attend the police academy brought uncertainty, loneliness, etc. and was easier to manage through alcohol consumption.

Why was it good?
When I was buzzed, I relinquished responsibility and blamed the alcohol.
After withdrawal I completely took on responsibility for my life and actually became more controlling. A shift to a new addiction?
I am more resilient than I ever thought I could be.
I have the ability to pull myself out of the deepest quagmire.
I am incredibly courageous!

My realization:
Alcohol does not liberate you; it merely hooks you.
No addiction can liberate you. It dangles an image of liberation in front of your nose until you finally realize you have a problem.
Alcohol removed me from myself.
Life without it has brought me closer to myself.
The closer I come to myself, the closer I can get to others (and let others in, too).

How am I doing today?
I am aware, but not anxious.
I am a role model for others.
I increasingly allow myself to be who I am.
I used to hide myself through alcohol. Today I show myself without it.

The Future:
For the past twenty-eight years I have been working as a volunteer in a self-help group for addicts. I run my own association. At the workplace I have emphasized the topic of alcohol and help other

addicts become sober. I want to continue to build out these tasks to create a second career on the side.

My offer:

Counseling, presentations, conversations. Offer potential solutions. Pass along information and offer assistance for self-help. Support and guiding through all issues that arise. Always with the approach that it is worth actively addressing the issue of alcohol dependency, to face these issues and to become healthy again and to make sense of your life again thanks tot he experiences you have had.

Further: to address the circumstances and behavioral patterns that strengthened the addiction and to remove their power.

There is good in everything ...
Without my battle with alcohol addiction I never would have had access to the wealth of experiences I do now.

The Happiest Moment in My Marriage

by Sabina F.

It has been eleven years and to this day I still cannot believe how incredibly unprepared one can be when something bad happens. It was a totally normal Wednesday in September, a day in which our world crumbled in an instant and I had to brace myself for the worst: the death of my husband.

My husband Alfred and I had a typical marriage with the normal highs and lows that come with it. That means that after eighteen years of marriage, one tends to live side-by-side, but not together. It didn't at all mean we did not love each other or were somehow indifferent. No, it was more that the organization of every day life took the helm and the intimacy and tenderness we once shared had paled.

At the time I worked as a receptionist for a large car dealership, a job which required a great deal of client contact, frequent returns and a lot of time spent on the phone. I had a demanding boss who expected me to be constantly friendly, patient and well manicured.

My husband Alfred worked as a sales representative for a pharmaceutical company. He was the top sales rep, earned well, but was constantly on the go and stood under a lot of pressure. When we was home, he essentially just wanted his peace and quiet so he could relax, take care of office matters and watch television. It sounds rather bleak, but I don't mean it that way. I always showed understanding for his professional situation, enjoyed the financial fruits of his labor and admired his ability to manage everything from our banking, insurance to the tax returns and new purchases in our home. Ours was a classic division of labor, but we liked the old-fashioned marriage we led. Although I have to admit I sometimes felt lonely and yearned for more emotion in our relationship.

On said Wednesday in September my cell phone rang multiple times, but there was so much going on at work that I wasn't able to check it. Later when two young police officers entered the car dealership and approached me, I knew right away that it had something to do with the cell phone calls I had ignored.

"Are you Mrs. Sabina F.?" one of the officers asked me. "Unfortunately, we have bad news. Your husband has collapsed and was brought to the hospital. But don't worry. He is alive. But you have to come with us right away. Your boss already knows. Please come with us and we'll explain everything."

With shaky knees I followed the police officers to their car where they told me what had happened. My husband had been in a sales discussion at a doctor's office when he suddenly collapsed. It was a blessing in disguise as the doctor most likely saved my husband's life. Alfred had had a severe heart attack and was currently undergoing an operation at the hospital.

When we arrived, I was led to the doctor on call along with the nurse in intensive care. They told me my husband would most likely not survive, but there was a slight chance he might. They had to review the situation and keep an eye on him. My husband would return from surgery in about one-half hour; they would know more then.

For the following thirty minutes, sitting in that small examination room neighboring the ER, I went through hell. Would my husband survive? How could a healthy, strong man who was only forty-five years old have such a severe heart attack? He had never had any physical ailments before. What was suddenly happening to us?

The longest thirty minutes of my life morphed into an entire hour of waiting before my husband returned from surgery. Even for a medical layperson such as myself, I knew it couldn't be good. The operating surgeon, however, offered a pretty good prognosis. They would leave him in intensive care for the next two or three days. I could visit him later when he was moved to the ward. The operation had gone well; they had given him a quadruple bypass and, for the time being, he was being given artificial respiration.

The first few days were the most critical, but it looked good. Most likely, my husband was going to survive.

I nearly fainted out of sheer relief, but the doctor wasn't finished with describing his condition. "Because of the severity of his heart attack, your husband is unconscious. It is actually a good thing for the body after such an incident and operation as it helps the body heal faster. It is the body's way of protecting itself. Unfortunately, we won't be able to give any reliable diagnosis about your husband's recovery or when he might regain consciousness. You have to be patient and think positive thoughts. Perhaps we can tell you more tomorrow."

I have no idea how I got home from the hospital that day. I also have no recollection about how I spent the rest of the day or the following night. I could neither eat nor drink anything. Nor could I sleep a wink. I fell into a state of desperation and hopelessness. I wanted to jump up and run back to the hospital because I was most certain that if my husband woke up, he would call out to me. I stared hypnotically at my cell phone, hoping that the hospital would suddenly call me and tell me my husband had awoken.

Somehow I managed to make it to the next morning until, at 7 a.m., I called a taxi to take me to the hospital. They received me with a great deal of warmth and expertise, used to dealing with family members confronted with extreme situations and trained to deal with the unnerved and desperate, as I was. They told me I could see my husband in a few hours, but everything looked good.

Given the circumstances, he had managed to pull through the night well.

Finally the time came for me to see my husband for the first time since his surgery. Strangely, I was calmed just by being able to be near him, even though he looked shattered and hooked up to so many beeping monitors, tubes and IVs. He looked so small, almost fragile in that hospital bed, and my husband is almost 5'11" and very athletic!

The doctor who was treating him couldn't give me any specific information about how long he would remain in his current condition. "Your husband could regain consciousness tonight – or maybe in a few days or even weeks." After a brief pause during which time he observed me closely to see how I took in his words and the sight of my husband in that bed, he added gently: "Be patient and keep the hope alive every day. Be optimistic! Your positive attitude can have an enormous effect on the patient. We can't explain it in traditional medical terms, but our experience tells us it is true: your husband will profit from both your presence and your optimism. Connect him with life; share everything happening around him with him. Talk to him; tell him about your day. Your husband will regain consciousness and return to you."

The doctor's words – albeit dramatic – unleashed a euphoric zest for action within me. I knew what to do! Of course I would shower my husband with attention and love to return him back to consciousness. I would talk so intimately with him that he would soon open his eyes and be the same old man I knew before this happened. I called my boss, who showed great understanding, and asked for time off work for as long as it would take to nurse my husband back to health. He told me not to worry about it and that everyone at the company was sending us many wishes for a speedy recovery. I will never forget how generous my boss was in that moment.

After just a few days, my initial optimism gave way to a deeper sense of depression and helplessness. Of course my husband didn't wake up that day, or the next one or even the next one. His condition remained stabile and the same as it had been.

You can't really imagine the feeling if you haven't experienced something like it before. What should you talk about with a person – and I mean hours at a time – whom you have known for twenty years and with whom you have shared a bed and your entire life? You would think you have shared enough experiences and that every day living would offer enough common topics of discussion. But: there was no conversation. As heartless as it may sound, I felt foolish, sitting there at my husband's bedside for hours at a time, holding senseless monologues without receiving a single reaction or response.

Luckily, I came up with a great idea that saved me. After spending an entire week, up to fifteen hours a day at my husband's bedside, the nurse resolutely sent me home with the promise that I would shower, eat something and sleep for a few hours. In that moment, I developed a new plan. If I began to run out of things to talk about, I would start reading aloud to my husband. Certainly, reading to him would also be a good way of communicating, right? The doctors and nurses agreed: "That's a great idea! Bring his favorite book or a magazine about a topic that would interest him. Cars? Sports? A business journal?"

Therein lies the rub. I had to admit that my husband never read books, just the daily paper and his company magazine. But it didn't matter. Perhaps it would be an opportunity to discover literature together. I went straight to the hospital library and picked out a good book that I liked to read out loud to give my husband new impulses. After scanning the shelves, I selected an English crime short stories – suspenseful, but not unnerving.

I started reading to my husband aloud the following day, but somehow I suddenly felt stupid. Was it not a dumb idea to read an English crime story out loud to my husband and to expect that he would regain consciousness that way? Could I somehow transfer positive impulses to my husband in this manner? Instinctively I knew it made no sense to engage in activities that I myself found stupid and helpless and still expect them to have a healing effect on my husband.

I was desperate. I had no ideas left. This could not be! Should my husband be damned to remain in this condition just because his wife has no imagination or idea – however crazy – about how to connect with him? Once again the understanding doctor stepped in to catch me in my emotional downfall: "Mrs. F., you desperately need a break. You are placing yourself under too much pressure.

Relax. Just keep your husband company. Hold his hand, but don't force yourself to do anything specific. Time will tell. Grant him your presence and love. That's enough for now."

I could have given the doctor a hug in that moment. He granted me so much relief and the ability to shake off the performance anxiety I had been feeling. The next day I actually enjoyed spending time in my husband's hospital room as I no longer fell the pressure to take action. I allowed myself to remain quiet and just sit next to him and look at him. The following day I asked the doctor's permission to bring in a small portable CD player so I could play music. I have to admit: it was in part because I was rather bored. I thought I could at least listen to a bit of music. I had selected a few French chansons, which I had taken from our CD collection at home. Alfred and I had gone on vacation to Brittany a long time ago. In the evenings while we were dining at a local restaurant, we had enjoyed the music so much that I would buy a CD before returning home to enjoy a few "French moments" in our every day lives. I would plan to cook a French meal. Alfred would open up a fantastic bottle of red wine and we would relive our vacation experience right at home.

But of course we never had a single "French evening". Our everyday lives quickly took hold. We never once listened to the CDs. Most of them were left unopened in the original packaging. As sad as the occasion was, we finally had the time to listen to the French chansons together. In reality it was only me who heard them, but whatever.

"We" listened to Charles Aznavour, Jacques Brel und mostly Charles Trenet. I took Alfred's lifeless hand and recalled one funny evening when we had gone to a so-called fine dining restaurant that everyone raved about only to find out that it was totally directed toward German tourists. They even had Wiener Schnitzel on the menu. We ate little, but drank two bottles of read wine, laughed and swayed arm in arm to Charles Trenet's Evergreen on the way home: "La mer... qu´on voit danser le long des golfes clairs …"

One late Friday evening after having been by Alfred's side until 9 p.m., I got a call from the hospital. I had listened to music with him, bought a sandwich at the kiosk and gone home to collapse on the couch. The sound of my telephone pierced through my bones. The hospital! Was something wrong with Alfred? I answered the phone with shaky hands. What the doctor told me was a complete shock! The doctor called me back to the hospital. My husband had opened his eyes for the first time shortly after I had left! He seemed disoriented and hadn't spoken a word, but his regaining consciousness was sensational progress.

I immediately called a taxi. When I arrived, I ran up the stairs to the ward and tore open the door to my husband's room without waiting for the doctor or nurse. The ward nurses and two doctors were standing in a semi-circle around his bed. They were beaming! My husband was oddly emotionless. He just lay there staring at me with big eyes. I suddenly didn't know how to act. Should I hug him? Would he know who I am? I stood at the door helplessly and looked at my husband. Once again the compassionate doctor saved the situation by saying: "Mr. F., I bet you are very happy to see your wife again and can hardly wait to hold her in your arms, right? It was your wife who brought you back through all the music she played."

At first my husband did not respond, then slowly turned his questioning eyes away from me and toward the doctor. "Yes. You most likely won't remember, but your wife entertained the entire ward with French chansons. Apparently the music is connected to a few romantic memories while you were both on vacation, right?"

Suddenly, my husband burst into tears. My energetic, rational, controlled, successful husband who used to find every sign of emotion an embarrassment! The first word he spoke with a soft voice was: "Sabina." He stretched out both arms toward me with a palpable yearning. To this day I cannot describe how I felt in that moment.

More importantly was what happened after my husband's release from the hospital and his ensuing recovery. He recovered relatively quickly, diligently went to every post-examination and was given a clean bill of health after just eight weeks from his hospital release date. He seemed quieter than before his heart attack, but also more pensive. I was excited about the newly woven intimacy that we shared. He would often give me a kiss as he walked by or would place his hand on mine at mealtime. We would spontaneously hug during the day. Our marriage has gained a depth and tenderness and a new quality about it. And it has remained so to this day.

An Unusual Encounter
by Oliver S.

It was shortly before my birthday and I had some time to kill. So why not take a whirl on my motorcycle?

I decided to take a mini-vacation to Lake Garda, as I often did. I quickly chose a small hotel in the mountains, then hopped on my bike. I awoke early on my birthday and looked out to the lake that was still enshrouded with the morning mist. Strolling through the hotel lobby after breakfast, I noticed a small wooden display case on the unmanned reception desk, which contained an Italian brochure. On the front it showed a church with an adjoining monastery.

Because I didn't know this part of Lake Garda, I decided to go there right away. After riding for a few miles along the serpentine roads, I saw a mountain lush with cypress trees on the right-hand side. I couldn't see anything behind it so I took off toward the direction of the mountain. As I reached the top, I was surprised to find the church I had seen on the brochure. The view below was breathtaking. As the morning mist slowly retreated, I could see the lake in all its glory in full view.

A large, locked wrought-iron gate showed the way to a steep, split set of stairs that led both left and right to the church entrance. In front of the entrance gate was a half-finished concrete terrace and the shell of a small café. As I sat down on the terrace to enjoy the view, I suddenly noticed someone behind me. A small elderly woman dressed completely in black smiled at me. Her smile was kind and warm, enhancing my already good mood.

"Good morning," I said, then added in jest, assuming she wouldn't understand me anyway, "All that's missing is an espresso." It took no more than fifteen seconds before the nice woman approached me again with a cup of espresso. I was amazed and tried to figure out how someone could make an espresso so quickly and – more importantly – where? There wasn't a kitchen to be found for miles, not to mention cooking facilities.

Suddenly the heavy wrought-iron gate stood open and the woman had disappeared. I hadn't heard a sound. I slowly walked up the steps to the church. The church door was wide open and the sun shined through the lateral windows, bathing the church's interior in a bright light.

All at once I saw the elderly woman again as she stood before the vestry, smiling warmly at me once again. I quickly ran to her, opening my wallet to reimburse her for the espresso. But the woman smiled, shaking her head and disappearing into the vestry. I placed a bank note in the donation box at the entrance and left the church twenty minutes later. After that, I rode my motorcycle aimlessly through the mountains. But for some reason I couldn't get the woman out of my mind.

Suddenly my cell phone rang. I stopped my bike and took the call. A good friend wanted to wish me a happy birthday. "What are you up to today? Can you believe I am in Lake Garda? When I am back home in Munich, let's get together, okay?"

"I'm in Lake Garda too – in Riva! Let's go out for dinner tonight."

I looked forward to our evening together. I was totally surprised by the coincidence. We met at a restaurant. As the food arrived, my friend casually asked me if I had anything to tell him, such as the woman with the espresso, the church and the amazing atmosphere surrounding it…

I nearly choked on my food. How on Earth could he have known? It was impossible! As I pressed him for information, he merely said: "That you'll have to find out for yourself."

On a side note, my friend is not a believer or spiritual in any way, shape or form. Quite the contrary! He is a very rational manager type for whom facts and numbers are the most important thing.

Dissatisfied and with no answers to my pressing questions, I returned to the hotel. The wooden display case at the reception desk had disappeared. I asked the night watchman, who spoke good English, where the brochure stand had gone. "What brochure stand?" he asked.

The next morning I asked the hotel manager about the brochure stand and his answer was the same as the night watchman's. I finally got the idea to look in my motorcycle jacket for the brochure I had placed there. When I looked, it wasn't there.

What happened that day is still a mystery to me. In the following years I visited the church twice. In the meantime the construction site had been removed. The café and the terrace had been finished. I never saw the elderly woman again. Several years ago I took my now wife to the mountains and proposed to her in front of the church. She said yes and we have been happily married ever since.

There are places and experiences that no one can rationally explain. And that's a good thing. Too often people are led only by their heads, not by their hearts. The church and monastery will always remain something special to me as well as the marriage proposal I made there that has brought me happiness ever since!

Four Best Friends
by Lisa N.

When I was a teenager, I had to repeat a grade because I had spent more time in nature than at my desk. Before the school year began that fall, I wondered what was in store for me.

On the first day of school, I entered my new classroom with great curiosity. The teacher sat me in the front row, most likely so he could keep an eye on me. At the time I went to an all girls' school with forty students in my grade. It would be no problem to make friends. I quickly came into conversation with my deskmate along with the girl sitting behind me. Her name was Felicitas, but everyone called her "Feli". Exchanging names was the first step in establishing our long-lasting friendship.

Feli and I became fast friends, but many of our classmates couldn't handle what we called our "special" sense of humor. Feli and I did a lot of things together such as our first dance class. As party time came around, we were the first to be there too.

At one of our friend's parties we met Hans, who was very good-looking. After the party, he drove us home. He dropped me off first as I lived outside of town. Then he took Feli home.

The following weekend in November 1981 it was party and disco time again. We decided to head for the most popular club in the city. We met Hans there, who introduced us to his best friend Alex.

Our friendship meant a lot to us both. Whenever we met guys, there was never a problem of jealousy as to who liked whom better. Such was the case this time too: it turns out Feli found Hans really attractive and I liked his friend Alex. At the time neither of us had a car. I had just turned eighteen and was studying to get my driver's license. Feli was only seventeen. As a result, we always had to rely on others to drive us home.

Because we lived in a rather small town, it was unavoidable to come across the same people over and over again. And so it was with our new friends Hans and Alex. On the weekends we would meet at the disco; during the week we'd see each other at the local cafés. When we first met, Alex was together with his long-time girlfriend who seemed to have her heart set on marrying him. But for him it wasn't an issue because he had just started a new sales job in the fashion industry. Hans had a long-time girlfriend too.

Both my girlfriend and I had just started vocational training. Feli wanted to become a hair stylist; I wanted to become a paralegal. It was a great period in our lives. We knew two really great young guys who were also both best friends and we did a lot of things together such as skiing and other excursions. When I finally passed my driver's education class, everything seemed to be perfect.

Feli and I yearned to have a set of wheels so it was awesome that Alex decided to sell me his second car, which was a Mini Cooper. Originally he had wanted to give it to his girlfriend, but she had seen me in it apparently and was no longer interested in the vehicle. Feli and I were finally free! Our first car – a red, hot Mini! I will never forget that tiny car.

After a time, Alex and his girlfriend broke up. She felt she had waited too long for him to propose. As a result, Alex and I met more and more often, spending a wonderful time together. But because he thought I was too young for a serious relationship, we broke it off after a year of back and forth. Feli and Hans were also no longer friends so she and I were now open for new adventures.

A few years later Alex married a model he had met during his job. His best friend Hans married his high school sweetheart.

Sounds like a perfect ending to the story, eh? Wait for it. You'll be surprised what life had in store for us all.

A few years passed. Relationships came and went. Feli fell in love and became pregnant with her son Benedikt. They married, then moved into a small house at the edge of town. I was so excited to be an "auntie" for her darling boy, for whom I was like a second mother. On Saturdays Feli would work in the hair salon with her mother so I would pick up the baby and take him shopping. We both enjoyed our afternoons together.

Unfortunately, Feli's marriage didn't last. After a few years, Feli moved back into her parents' house. Her mother was a proud grandma, happy to have her grandson close to her. As a result, Feli was able to work a lot more and finally took over the hair salon from her mom. Her son was in the best of care at home with his grandma.

At the time I too had had a rather rocky two-year relationship. Although I was still very young, I had the sense to recognize that a relationship with someone who suppresses you the entire time has no future. My parents were always by my side, offering me a soft place to land at home and always willing to lend an ear when I needed it. They never blamed me. I always knew that no matter what happened, they would be on my side.

There we were again, Feli and I, as freshly separated single women on the town again. It did us a world of good to go out rather than hide at home at our parents' houses. Sure, we met a few guys, but no one seemed to be a real match for either one of us. One night after coming home from work, my mother told me someone had called for me, a certain Alex. At first I didn't know whom she meant as I knew a few young men with that name, but I was puzzled as to which one would have called me.

I called the number, only to be surprised that it was the Alex whom I had met all those years ago with Hans. After a little small talk, he asked me if I still worked at the law office. I immediately thought it had to do with a liability case or some other lawsuit. But his answer was another: "It's about divorce." "Who is getting a divorce?" I asked. "I am."

His words moved me to the core. "Try to see if you can make it work. Marriage is a wonderful thing. You shouldn't end it just like that," I advised him.

Through my work in the law office I was very familiar with the war of the roses that divorce could bring. But when it happened to friends, it was a different story.

Because I had plans to go out with Feli, I quickly ended the call with Alex and told him to contact me at the law office on Monday.

I couldn't stop thinking about it. I mean I had seen him around town over the years, which is unavoidable when you live in small town, but somehow hearing from him made my heart race.

Later that night when I met Feli at our local hangout, I told her the news. She wasn't surprised. She was certain Alex and I would find our way back to each other. When he showed up at the bar that same evening, my old feelings flared up. Certainly I was a few years older and more mature now. Our five-year age difference wasn't that big a deal anymore.

We talked a long time that night, then he brought me home. We met the following day and reestablished our connection. His soon-to-be ex-wife had left him for another man from whom she was pregnant. My boss, a well-known divorce lawyer, made sure the whole thing was handled quickly.

Alex was free again, but the marriage, or rather the way in which it ended, weighed heavily upon him. He and his wife had gotten married in Hawaii. It had been a fairytale wedding. I knew the aftershock of his marriage would last a while.

At first I couldn't image starting a serious relationship with him because most of our conversations centered on memories of his ex-wife. He constantly compared me to her. Whenever we would vacation at a place where they had both been, it would stir up memories for him.

At first it was really hard for me, but I soon realized how much he meant to me. He exuded the kind of warmth and goodness I had never experienced in another man. We talked about everything and the trust between us kept growing.

My private life was humming along beautifully. I was extremely happy. Although my job at the law office was interesting, I decided to make a change after having worked there for eight years. A lot of my decision had to do with my boss' wife who made everyone's life difficult. After a year of night school where I got my executive secretary license, I wanted to start a new career path.

An acquaintance of mine had a real estate office and was in search of a secretary. After quitting the law office, I applied for the job, which I got immediately due to my level of experience. At the time I was still living with my parents. My mother suggested that, in my mid-20s, it might make sense for me to get my own apartment. I certainly could afford to move into my own four walls, a small, yet elegant place in the middle of town.

Things were going really well with Alex. He moved out of his marital abode and looked for a new place. We visited each other often and our relationship grew closer by the day. At the same time we thought it was too early for us to move in together. I was clear that he needed to find himself again after his failed marriage before leaping into the next live-in relationship.

Feli and I kept in contact after all those years. Our friendship was an important part of my life. Feli knew Alex in the past when he was out on the town with his best friend Hans. Hans' marriage, which had started in Hawaii, too, had limited his circle of friends. He rarely kept in touch with his best friend Alex because Hans' wife knew that they had gone out with Feli and me on numerous occasions. Jealousy reigned.

After our four-year relationship, which was extremely harmonious and trusting, Alex and I decided to get married. Because he had already been married before and I absolutely wanted to a church wedding, I went to city hall to ask if it was possible. It turns out his first marriage in Hawaii had ever been recognized by the German authorities, making his divorce completely irrelevant too. No lawyer or judge could substantiate that. But we were able to have a church wedding, which was the main thing. It was a dream come true for me. We chose a small pilgrimage church in the mountains and asked Hans and Feli to be our best man and bride's maid.

It was the most beautiful day of my life. My father walked me down the aisle and handed me to Alex, saying, "I have been there for Lisa for the past thirty years. Now it's your turn. Please take good care of her!"

The pastor was an old schoolmate of ours, which made it that much more personal. Our families, brothers and friends accompanied us along our path. And Benedikt, Feli's then three-year-old son, was the flower boy.

After the wedding we spent our honeymoon with a married couple from the fashion industry with whom we were very close. At some point we made a joke about my entering the industry. But I was happy with my current office job and couldn't imagine switching to one in the fashion world. Somehow I couldn't get the thought out of my mind so I decided to reduce my office job hours to four days a week and spent one full day helping Alex in his company. That way I was able to gain insights into the industry to determine whether it was a good fit for me.

After a year of marriage, I was amazed when Alex' company offered me a position to represent their women's line. It was an enormous opportunity for me. Although I had been happy in my old job, I had the feeling my husband needed me. After giving myself two weeks to think about it and writing down all the pros and cons, I informed my boss that I was leaving. At first he offered me twice my salary, but that couldn't stop my decision. It wasn't about money, but rather about my relationship with my husband. Alex was thrilled about my decision to begin working full-time together.

Shortly thereafter his best friend Hans told us he was moving to New York with his wife. We celebrated their farewell party, then brought them to the airport. Although they had had a tight friendship, the distance between Germany and the US was enormous. It was no longer possible to have a casual drink and the time difference made talking on the phone much more difficult.

We decided to celebrate New Year's Eve with them in New York. We noticed right away that his wife had completed closed the chapter on Germany and we felt oddly out of place. As a result, we packed our bags on New Year's Day and headed for the sunshine in Miami for the rest of our vacation.

At the time Feli lived with her son and new boyfriend. Nonetheless she was always up to date as to what was going on with Hans in New York. He would visit Germany at least once a year to see his parents and stop by Feli's house, even though she remained reserved toward him. Both of them were in relationship with someone else.

Unfortunately, Hans' marriage also failed and his wife returned to Germany to live with her parents. I had observed the situation for a long time. It was clear to me that both of our best friends were made for each other. The question was how they would find a way to each other.

When Hans returned to Germany for Christmas, we planned a weekend at a cabin in the mountains. We wanted other friends to join us so we spontaneously invited Feli and Hans. We spent a lovely time together and noticed that sparks flew between Hans and Feli. But unfortunately, neither one was ready to admit it.

Over New Year's Eve Alex and I celebrated with Hans alone in Munich. That evening it was so obvious that Hans had strong feelings for Feli. But he was blocked due to her other relationship. Something had to happen fast. Shortly before his departure, we invited both for a mutual evening in Munich. The four of us went out to dinner, chatting all the while. As I recall, that was the defining moment for both of them as the sparks continued to fly.

When Hans had to return to the US the next day, Feli was extremely sad. They started a long-distance relationship for a few years, until his job situation required he move from the East to the West coast. Because of the time zone challenges, he asked Feli if she could imagine moving to Los Angeles with him. She took the chance and agreed.

For years now both of our best friends live in the US. We are always very happy to see each other. We visit them in the US almost every year and they come for Christmas. Of course, the time difference presents its own set of challenges. We usually talk on the phone at night our time. But our friendship has always been about quality, not quantity.

Feli's son Benedikt is also happy about their relationship. He lives his own life in Germany, but knows that his mother is always there for him. Besides, he has an "alternate Mommy" in me.

A lot of friendships fade with time or fall apart. The four of us are very proud of ours! After many years, Alex and I found a way to each other as did our best friends Feli and Hans.

We will never forget how it all started – that moment in time when two schoolgirls met a good-looking man named Hans at a party …

A Life-Changing Decision
by Richard A.

When I closed my fabric store at the end of December 1991 after many years as a successful businessman, I was faced with how my professional future might look.

During my four-week closeout sale right before Christmas, I was approached by a loyal customer who asked if I might be interested in working at his company. In response to my question about what the job might entail, he told me I would be selling tax-advantaged real estate as well as life insurance and the like.

We agreed upon a six-month probationary period during which time I could get a feel for the job. After a relatively short time, I realized the job wasn't for me. For one, I had to attend numerous seminars. In addition, I was required to work nights and weekends to visit clients in order to sell them life, health and casualty insurance.

After just four months, I ended our working relationship and was faced once again with the question as to what I should do next. Should I return to the textile industry or try something entirely new. What should I do?

After going back and forth in my mind, my younger brother suggested that I accompany him to the next large tradeshow "Ambiente" in Frankfurt, Germany. He had worked as an independent sales representative for the interior design industry, traveling around Bavaria for his work. "You might be able to find a position as a sales rep in the area of giftware at the world's largest consumer trade show," he said.

At first I objected. "It's easy for you to say. You are well established in your job, but for me it's new ground!" He countered me by saying it would be possible to get ahold of a list complied by the trade association for independent sales reps in which a bunch of companies looking for field reps in certain regions appeared.

And so it was that I found myself accompanying my brother to Frankfurt to research a potential sales job. Straight away on Saturday I went to the trade association's office to get the list with the job offers available. The task was harder than I thought. You have to know that at that time – at the start of the '90s -- the trade show ran across twelve enormous halls that each contained four floors.

List in hand, I went at it, searching for companies in the various halls and levels that were looking for sales reps for giftware of all kinds. Due to my total lack of experience in the field, I had no idea how to identify whether the job was good, bad or just simply boring.

I went from hall to hall and booth to booth from 8 a.m. until 6p.m. without any success. Either they were looking for sales reps for entirely new territories that had yet to be developed or the wares they were selling seemed completely unmarketable.

Upon my return to my brother's booth that evening, he and his colleagues told me, based on their own experience and for various reasons, to completely forget the companies I had looked at. So there I stood, empty-handed with sore feet and nothing to show for it.

That evening I went with my brother into the center of town in Frankfurt to grab a bite to eat at a cozy restaurant with some of his colleagues and neighboring booth mates. My feet stopped throbbing. Just as I was about to order my third beer out of sheer frustration about the day I had had, the man sitting across from me asked me what I did for a living. Nothing at the moment, I admitted to him. It turns out he ran one of the most successful Hanseatic tea import companies in the world.

I found myself telling him about my professional background and about my efforts to find an appropriate sales job, but that I had come up empty-handed. Without blinking an eye he told me quite spontaneously about a possible position he knew of. He said that, should his suggestion materialize into a full-blown position, I had to promise to pay him a commission by giving both his kids Christmas gifts for the rest of my life. I was hooked.

When I asked him what type of sales job it was, he told me it would be with a Hamburg-based import business that imports Christmas and Easter items along with glass, porcelain and other items from China. I didn't have a clear picture of the position in my mind, but the nice man offered to introduce me to the company's CEO the very next day anyway.

At nine o'clock sharp the next morning as the tradeshow opened, we stood in the company's 320 square foot booth. After a brief introduction, my acquaintance excused himself, leaving me alone with the CEO of the import company. As my gaze swept across the booth, I had to ask myself what I had gotten myself into? The booth's appearance confused the daylights out of me. I saw a collection of Christmas angels, Santa Clauses, snowmen, decorative storm lamps, Easter bunnies, lawn ornaments, figures made of porcelain and ceramic, etc. It looked like a shooting gallery!

Oh my lord! And I would have to sell this stuff? How could I even make a living doing this? I wrung my hands in desperation. I much preferred the large, tastefully and elaborately decorated booths nearby.

Back to my conversation with the CEO. I told him about my professional experience including my formal education that included a sales apprenticeship, a degree from a textile design school, my experience working in my parents' fashion retail store along with my own freelance work and my brief "excursion" into the insurance and real estate industry.

One thing I noticed during our chat was the fact that his booth filled up with people the moment the tradeshow floor was opened while the more stylish booths surrounding him remained empty.

The CEO asked me to go to the shelf with the ceramic figurines. More specifically, he asked me to pick up one of the two-inch hand-painted Christmas angels and guess what it might cost. "Between two and three dollars," I estimated. The CEO's chest ballooned with pride. "Nope. Just fifty cents!" The price wasn't for a single angel, but for a set of four. Four pieces for fifty cents! And they were to be sold in a cardboard box. One box contained 288 sets of four. His clients were wholesalers, furniture stores, garden centers, mail order businesses, Christmas markets, chain stores that sold gifts and much, much more.

I have to admit I was impressed. We engaged in some more chitchat before the CEO told me to come back at 2 p.m. so I could meet one of the managers from Hamburg. We could then go from there.

My mood soaring, I found my way back to my brother's stand. I told him and his colleagues about the potential new position. They had only good things to say about the Hamburg-based company.

I told my brother I had another appointment at 2 p.m. to discuss the details with the head of the company. He offered to accompany me in order to lend his support during the conversation.

At exactly 2 p.m. we appeared at the booth of the Hamburg-based company. In the meantime the booth was packed with clients. Every single representative and employee was busy consulting their clients and sealing deals. We got to know the head of the company with whom my brother and I, along with the CEO, engaged in an animated conversation about how we might work together.

We soon came to an agreement that it was worth a try. They suggested that the head of the company contact me at the beginning of October so I could come to Hamburg to sign the contract. Furthermore, they had to come to a settlement agreement with the sales rep who had been in charged of the Bavarian territory up to now. When I asked why he was leaving, they told me that he had decided of his own volition and that he himself was sorry to leave, even though the company had been very happy with his performance.

The father of three daughters, the man was leaving because he had undergone gender reassignment. It had been a long time coming. They told me that his sales territory in Catholic Bavaria wouldn't tolerate seeing a man, then a woman in the same sales rep, not to mention the enormous psychological and physical tolls it took after making such a decision.

At first I was a little shocked, but as it often is in life, my predecessor's life-changing decision also altered my own professional future.

It was clear that the company would wait until October to contact me because they needed to settle everything with the former sales rep. Shortly before I left their booth, I commented on how busy their booth was. The company head took one look at me and said I could get started right away as there were a lot of clients from Bavaria at the booth.

I didn't hesitate for a second, grabbing a packet of contracts and a pen to get started. I had planned to stay until the end of the tradeshow anyway and had plenty of time. By the look on his face, the head of the company was pleased with my go get 'em attitude. The rest of the tradeshow was fascinating. It offered me an opportunity to become familiar with the company's processes and my co-workers too.

At the end of the show on Tuesday evening, my brother and I returned to Munich. I now had to wait until I got the call from Hamburg. As promised, the head of the company called me at the beginning of October and asked me to come to Hamburg to take care of the formalities.

A week later I found myself in a train headed to Hamburg. A company employee picked me up at the train station and brought me to headquarters. After a warm reception by the employees and management and a quick look around the place, we got down to business by mutually agreeing on a six-month probationary period as a sales representative.

Of course I had to get used to the territory in Bavaria at first, but after just a few appointments with clients and a handful of tradeshows, I quickly got the swing of things. Headquarters in Hamburg offered me tremendous support. It was the beginning of a wonderful, successful cooperation that has lasted twenty-one years.

It was the Year 1954
by Maria P.

At the age of nineteen, I was working in a large department store in the catering department. The store held a grand opening with a ton of invited guests and clients. Even the mayor and numerous celebrities showed up to help celebrate the occasion. There was a lot of work to do in preparation for the event to ensure everything was just right. We were also responsible for pulling off the event itself. Finally, at 3 a.m. after the festivities had ended, we were allowed to go home.

An elderly colleague was concerned about how I might get home so he suggested sharing a taxi with a new employee. The company would pay for it.

No sooner said than done! The "new guy" was a very good-looking thirty-five year old man. As a young girl, I must say I had a lot of respect for him. After the taxi he called arrived, we had a nice conversation during the taxi ride. He told the taxi driver to take me home first, then continued on to his own house.

The next day at the office he approached me and jokingly said: "You know I think I may have deserved a goodnight kiss last night after accompanying you home last night…"

I joked back, saying, "Now you think of it! It's rather brazen of you to approach me now when it's too late!" He smiled. "What can I say? I'm a little slow?!"

He winked at me. "Just wait. One day I won't be so slow!"

From that point on a group of us at work hung out together and slowly, but surely, he and I grew closer. Until one day I suddenly realized: He's the one!

We were a happy couple who got along very well. However, four years later he became very ill and had to undergo surgery twice. He wasn't doing well at all and I was very worried about him. Every night after work I would sit by his bedside, care for him and try to raise his spirits.

Then one night out of the blue he said: "You are the greatest woman I have ever met. I love you from the bottom of my heart. Let's get married!"

With great joy I told him yes: "And you are the greatest love of my life."

His illness was a blessing in disguise. We were married for fifty-three years, have two wonderful children who later married wonderful people too that made our joy complete. Today as a widow living on her own, I am an extremely happy person who had the most wonderful man and father of my children. His love meant everything.

Like Phoenix From the Ashes

by Loui Zinnober

I remember the day, that crystal-clear moment, when my entire life changed – in a flash. Literally!

You would normally only allow people to describe the experience who actually remember it happening. It wasn't the case for me, which is quite a shame because I imagine it must have been a spectacular moment in time: two electric shocks and a clap of thunder, followed by fire and smoke.

Big-time stuff.

And I was the lead actor in this short, yet violent drama. It was an enormous, spooky departure from my "first life". My "second life" began thereafter. It was a long, difficult and painful rebirth.

It was a sunny Sunday at the beginning of spring. I had a date with friends. Everyone was in the best of spring-like moods. We decided to take a walk.

The supporting actors: me, seven buddies, a woman and a German shepherd. The location: meadows, an athletic field, the edge of the forest, a railway yard.

At the edge of the forest we climbed relatively high trees. Amongst all our chatting and frolicking we reached the railway yard. At the time I had a strong need to be the center of attention in these types of situations. I wanted to be the main entertainer and acted like the class clown. The little trees and the hunter's stand I had climbed – much to my friend's amusement – got me riled up. I was enthralled by the view of the seemingly endless line of freight cars below.

At this point, I must interject that it was a time when a few of my friends and I had a promising vision of becoming railway vagabonds. Or a pop star. Or something along those lines.

Such crazy thoughts are pretty typical for thirteen-year-old boys. But I had just celebrated my seventeenth birthday. So as you can see I was a bit of a late bloomer and harbored enigmatic romantic yearnings. We were a bunch of big kids, cigarettes dangling from our big mouths. With a beer in one hand and with plans of grandeur in our heads. It was a wonderful period in my life.

I simply didn't want to part – nor could I really – from my romantic visions. Luckily, I was able to turn those yearnings into a career. But more on that later.

Back at the railway yard I was electrified by the view of these massive behemoths made of iron and steel. It was odd really – exactly two weeks prior on a beautiful spring Sunday, I had spent time at the exact place with a few of my friends. We had climbed one of the freight cars, a so-called "flat car". As the name suggests, it had a flat build, allowing for a lot of "ceiling room" to transport containers, automobiles and the like. I only mention it because this particular detail is important to the story.

During our first visit we had viewed the place as "safe" and as a "playground". It was a "playground" of sorts. But, of the most dangerous kind.

We had reached these cars again, but this time there were no "flat cars", but rather "open bulk cargo wagons". The contrast between the two would soon become apparent to me. The bulk cargo wagons were impressive giants, at least sixteen feet high. They were enormous, something of which a future railway vagabond could only dream. They were a worthy opponent for a young hero whose future was shiny and bright. As with the others, the blue spring sky radiated upon these cars. I noticed, however, that the "ceiling room" cars enjoyed less sunlight. Wait for it.

As I climbed the railway embankment, I noticed a beautiful, slim iron ladder on the side of the car. It couldn't have been more inviting for me – a sure thing as we like to say in Bavaria. After a few steps, I began to "climb the rigging" as mariners call it. I carried a leather dog leash with massive iron carabiners on my shoulder. I threw myself up onto the ladder like a monkey and, step for step, with great arrogance and a zest for life, I climbed toward my new life. But first, I had to end my old life, which happened fast.

You can easily guess what happened to me next, the seemingly eternal jokester. At the time, however, I experienced what it must feel like to be a pop star who is about to walk on stage. I even had an audience: a few of my buddies watched my capers with amusement. On top of it, it was springtime. I was full of arrogance and levity…When I got to the edge of the car, I lifted myself up from my kneeling position with the dog leash in my left hand and wanted to make a loud announcement, using the carabiners as my alternative "microphone". Looking down at the astounded faces of my friends sixteen feet below me, I couldn't know that that image would be the last one I would see for a while. Sunday afternoon, shortly before 3 p.m.

Above me a light went on and within me the lights went out…

It took me a long time to piece together the rest of that day from bits of my memory and from others' descriptions. It took over a year before I could completely remember that dark day. The so-called "moment that changed my life forever" isn't something I experienced, but rather something I survived. I only know it from the stories my friends told me later about that particular, horrible moment that they had to witness and certainly will never forget.

As I was lifting myself up on the edge of the wagon, two electric shocks hit me. One went directly through my left hand.

The other went straight through my skull. It's easy to guess how it happened. The two electric shocks came from a power line that runs through most train tracks. I still can't believe after all these years how I could have been so blind and careless. How could I have not given it any thought about how dangerous and insane my actions were? Not once did I look up as I climbed the car so for me the power line was nonexistent. Two weeks prior it had all been so "safe and like a playground." That was it.

It is especially noteworthy to mention that I of all people was the one to do such an insane thing. Quite honestly, I wasn't even a daredevil. I was much more the clown! On that note, it was indeed something I would do. It was such an unbelievably beautiful day. My whole life lay before me. I was intoxicated by the feelings of spring and simply euphoric. The cloudless sky hung above my head, below stood an entire audience that looked up to me.

And yet what compelling reasons does a seventeen-year-old kid need to do the dumbest things? Where was I now? Oh yes. The power lines.

Two electric shocks: one through my skull, the other through my hand. Because I was holding carabiners made of iron and both legs were planted firmly on a mountain of iron and steel, the electric currents ran through me like a waterfall. The entry hole was my skull; the exit hole was the sole of my foot.

The effect was massive: you have to give electricity credit for that. I was propelled into the open car with an enormous force and suddenly vanished into thin air. Everyone who saw the accident was paralyzed and in total shock. Simultaneously, you could hear a loud explosive noise as the currents ran through my body. Even at that moment, no one realized the power lines were the cause for the disaster. Years later it moved me to tears as I remembered that I was an avid reader of old stories at the time. I was especially enthusiastic about Greek, Roman and Germanic mythology and stories of heroism. The story of Zeus excited me most as he took out his thunderbolt and pulverized some naughty sinner. I was so passionate about these stories that on some level I found comfort in having been electrocuted instead of having been run over by a drunk driver, for instance. I didn't feel like a "victim," but rather a "perpetrator" because I had taken action!

Making lemons out of lemonade in the hardest of times is what one does to survive.

Let's go back once again to the railway car because there is another course in the menu of this juicy story. You can see how much electricity a railway power line has when you are at a railroad crossing and observe a locomotive pulling a line of seemingly never-ending railway cars. Thousands of tons of machines, stones, wood, chemical tanks, etc. Apparently, it requires 15.000 Volt, 16 2/3 Hz. Now that's shocking!

To this day I have no idea about the subject matter. But it must be a lot of voltage because the energy of it generated such an enormous amount of heat that it set my clothes on fire. Unconscious and ablaze, I lay atop a sixteen-foot high railway car.

My friends stood at the edge of the embankment, paralyzed with horror. No one knew what had actually happened and they couldn't see me, except for my right leg that hung from the edge of the car and was surround by flames and smoke. I lay burning on the car. They only saw the smoke that slowly arose from the car.

Whenever I think about what happened next, I am still very moved and touched by it after all these years. Two of my friends climbed up the freight car to see what had happened to me. When they peered over the ledge of the car, they way me lying there like a pile of dirt, aflame and nearly dead. The distance between the car and the power line was about three feet. If you realize that it only takes the distance of four feet to unleash an electric shock from a power line, then you will know my two friends were in the same danger I had been. But neither of them thought about the power line that hung over their heads like the sword of Damocles. They extinguished the fire with a jacket.

And not a minute too late. There wasn't a part of me that was left unscathed. I had third and fourth degree burns on my arms, torso, arms, hands and head. My greatest fortune is that my friends didn't have to pay for their heroic efforts with their lives!

In the meantime, people from a neighboring soccer field had gathered after hearing the explosion that the electric shock had created. Risking their lives, two of the soccer players climbed up the car and helped me down. Luckily, there were no more electric currents running through the power line so that they too were left unharmed as they selflessly saved my life.

On this Sunday afternoon another miracle beyond my own survival occurred: my rescuers survived too.

I now lay on the green meadow, in very bad condition with my charcoaled jeans and t-shirt. The smell of burned flesh, hair and textiles surrounded me. After a few minutes, I slowly opened my eyes, not knowing what had happened to me. I noticed that one of my friends knelt next to me and tried to talk calmly to me. Although I was only awake for a short while, I knew something horrible must have happened to me. I felt a strong, dull ache in my leg and a profound fear of death overcame me, which was only made worse by the sight of the gawking crowd encircling me. At the same time, I started making vacation plans with my friend for our forthcoming summer break.

Suddenly, slurring more than speaking, I said to my buddy: "I know I have to die, but I don't want to!" It was a strange statement, almost even funny, a trace of megalomania, considering my current condition.

I believe it was a life-saving statement.

Not because it smacked of heroism or revealed something great about me. Certainly not. But somewhere deep down within me, I knew what it meant and something clung to the final threads of my tiny existence that wanted to live.

What followed was the usual procedure: emergency doctor, helicopter, burn care facility. In the days that followed, it became clear about the extent of my catastrophe. Amnesia and, in short, I was nearly totaled like a car on the autobahn. Chances of survival: nearly zero.

Fifteen months later I was still alive. They handed me a pair of crutches and released me from the hospital. For me it didn't feel like fifteen months, but rather thousands of years.

Thousands of years of pain, fear and desperation. I was a young man without hope, but with a lot of yearning for my home, my friends, parties and girls…

Somewhere along the line after being home for a time, I slowly began to realize that I would never "come home" again. My childhood was over and I was no longer the person I was when I embarked on that walk with friends on Sunday afternoon in springtime.

The doctors and caregivers did extraordinary work, showing great commitment and knowledge as they fought for my life. The story happened in the '70s, Back then emergency medicine wasn't at the same level it is today and they certainly had less to work with to save the lives of the severely injured. Up to that point, I didn't have a particularly physically or psychologically sound constitution, but apparently I was blessed with a rather robust nature.

A lot of things must have come together that allowed me to survive that inferno. You could start to imagine what it might be…

Why me?

The best antidote for senseless thoughts is to turn them around and say, for instance:

Why *not* me?

Why do you always think that the bad news you hear on the television or in police reports only pertains to everyone else but you? A series of other ghosts haunt me such as the thought that God somehow wished to punish me. Or does he have something great in store for me? More often than not, I had to force myself to move away from those dark thoughts and toward the light of decision-making and action.

Pretty soon it was clear that my "new life" offered a great deal of challenges for me – every day, every hour. It wasn't just a question of "to be or not to be," but rather "walking" or "wheelchair".

The first step was to learn how to walk again. I was on crutches for two solid years. I also had to regain the use of my left hand that nearly had to be amputated after being electrocuted. Rolling my own cigarettes certainly helped!

And of course I had a serious need to make up for lost time by engaging in all kinds of pleasurable activities for which I put my very best foot forward. It was the mother of all questions: what will happen next to this survival artist?

Artist?
Artist!

Exactly!

Up to the "Day of Fire" I had never really made any concrete plans for my career path. Why should I? I mean the sun shined every day, life was basically pleasant and sometimes even wonderful. I had plenty of friends, not to mention all those pretty girls.

In certain dreamy moments when I would turn my thoughts to my professional future, I typically had pipe dreams filled with images, art, freedom and adventure.

Those days filled with sweet dreams had long gone and had been replaced by an icy cold wind. In the interim, I had finished high school. The humanists in my Latin school had ushered me out of their noble halls and I now stood before an abyss! Nothing else stood in the way of my path as an "artist". Sure, I had doubts about my prospects for success in my undertakings, but I was also convinced that I had found my true home in the world of imposters, nutcases and babblers.

Going to work every day, even if it had gotten late – or rather early – at the bar the night before, was now my goal! And I achieved that goal, even if it frequently took a lot of effort to fight the devil inside me.

Even though the first few years were extremely difficult after my new life began, I managed to establish a routine and regained my footing. After a time, I was even able to earn some money from the pictures I drew. After a few failed college applications, I was even accepted to the art academy in Munich where I spent the next six years before graduating with my master's degree. What a beautiful, senseless piece of paper! But what did make sense were all the things I learned while at the academy. Because I had a clear idea of what I wanted out, I was able to approach my studies with a great deal of focus and ambition. Nude drawings, print graphics and scientific drawings were a part of my self-made schedule. I spent years intensely studying various painting techniques.

In retrospect, it was a good investment in my future. My education afforded me a great deal of insight into the use of raw materials and techniques that gave me a leg up in my profession. It also exposed me to a broad spectrum of artistic expression.

It has been almost forty years since that beautiful spring day on which my youth went up in smoke and flames. The "railway vagabond" lives on and with great pleasure most of the time. I am one of the lucky ones that gets to do what he loves, which in my case is painting, drawing and photography. And I'm not bad at it. I have never tried to suppress or forget the memories of that horrible time in my life. Thank God! Sometimes I think about what a hopeless and pitiful state I was in as they loaded me onto the helicopter. I have to laugh when I think about how great my life is now.

I'm serious even though I will continue to pay a high price until the end of my days for my "first ascent" onto that railway car.

I have no idea how my life would have turned out if I had not had that crazy idea to climb up on that car. Maybe-perhaps-probably it would have been a quieter life indeed.

But would it have been a better one? I don't think so. I also don't believe – without trying to sound too woo-woo – that it happened "by accident". It wasn't "pre-determined" or anything like that. I have simply always tended toward tragicomic and adventuresome experiences. My way was always been a winding, non-linear road.

It creaks and groads above and below deck, but that old ship is still cruising along the ocean. The now greying captain tells his sometimes childish, but always vivid cock-and-bull stories and hopes to have enough water under his keel.

I continue to go through life as a "branded painter" who is occasionally a bit unsteady on his feet, but still standing strong with a million colorful and black and white images in his head along with an enormous, endless reservoir of ideas, dreams and yearnings. I believe I am well equipped with my knapsack in har to spin around the world multiple times!

The gods, those eternal beings,
give the favored everything,
All joy, those eternal beings,
All pain, those eternal beings,
Everything.
JOHANN WOLFGANG VON GOETHE

Never Lose Yourself
by Anna D.

The pace of our lives today has grown incredibly fast. You see it in the daily news in which dramatic shifts can happen in an instant. Despite all our access to modern technology, we are constantly confronted by our own fragility and the dangers lurking everywhere.

My story begins long, long ago. At the tender age of seventeen as World War II was about to end, I found myself fleeing Silesia. Our goal was to reach Freiburg, Germany. In subzero temperatures, we stood five in a row on the trains to secure room and a path to freedom. We managed to sit on one side of the car with the other refugees while our luggage sat on the other.

When we finally reached the West, we were forced to make a bitter realization: our relatives weren't exactly thrilled about our arrival. Soon we departed for another place. We set our sights on the Austrian town of St. Wolfgang. On the left-hand side of the lake was the Russian occupied zone; on the right-hand side were the Americans. Luckily, I had a command of the English language thanks to my good education. As a result, my mother and I were able to find shelter in the American barracks. We found a job in the kitchen. When the refugees were sent away, the American commander said to us: "You can stay here."

One day we met a man on the street who was headed to Germany. He was responsible for transporting machine parts there so we hitched a ride and found ourselves in a refugee camp in Schweinfurt. The American commander had written a reference for us, which allowed us to travel further to Heidelberg where we found shelter in an empty hotel.

The whole time we were haunted by the burning question as to the whereabouts of my father. We finally got word that he was in the Czech Republic where he had collapsed while fleeing from the Russians. He was a diabetic. Luckily, we were able to send insulin via my mother's brother, but somehow it never arrived. Shortly thereafter, we discovered he had died.

After the war, we had to learn to fight for our basic needs. Because my zodiac sign is a "Taurus", I found it easy to assert my opinion and to stand up for what I believed in. Our fleeing had found an end after the war when we finally found a home in Munich. It was there that I met my husband, a physicist who was working in the research department of a large German company.

The years that followed were happy ones. We had a healthy little girl, who later went to school and college. My husband had always dreamed of travel after retirement. When he was offered the possibility of early retirement, he lunged at the chance. And once again destiny had us firmly in its grip. Not a year later he became very ill and died the following year. He was sixty-five years old.

It was a painful loss indeed. Thanks to my prior training as a cosmetician and pedicurist, I was able to open up a salon in a nursing home with the help of two assistants. At the age of sixty-five, however, I had a stroke and had a bad fall while getting out of the car.

For the past ten months I myself have been in a nursing home, but I feel very good here. Never once did I give up, nor did I fear life's difficulties. I think we have to make the best of things because we only have this one life.

Let us be thankful for that which we have in life and not complain about that which we do not.

An Unbelievable Discovery
by Paul B.

For years my wife and I had one wish: to go on an adventure trip through Alaska with a mobile home for once in our lives!

We finally realized our dream in August of 2014, embarking on a trip of a lifetime. At the end of our first travel day, we headed for the idyllic "Eagle River Campground" with our pick-up camper, securing a campsite for our stay.

To our delight we discovered we had two lovely neighbors at the campground: an elderly married couple named Bob and Marie. These two adventuresome Americans, seventy-three and sixty-seven years old, originated from New Hampshire on the East Coast of the United States, but they had called Anchorage, Alaska, their home for years now. They had been married a total of fifty-one years. The amazing thing was that they had married so young. Bob had been twenty-two and Marie had been just sixteen!

One evening while we barbecued amidst the overwhelmingly beautiful landscape, they both told us the craziest story.

For years Bob had been an avid treasure hunter, having tirelessly scoured various historically fascinating places with his metal detector. His brother, who had passed away just two years prior, had shared his passion for treasure hunting with Bob. His dream had been to finally find a rare fifty cent piece, but he was never able to do so.

But just that day on which the four of us sat together on this magnificent campground near the Eagle River in Alaska, Bob had finally found his fortune with his metal detector – a fifty cent piece that was lying near their camper.

The amazing part was that the coin came from the year 1954, the exact year in which Bob had come to Alaska with his brother! Bob told us the story with tears in his eyes, saying he would give the coin to his deceased brother by placing it in the urn where his ashes lay.

To this day we still think fondly about Bob and Marie, that lovely couple from Alaska and their incredible discovery. It's a story that truly moved us!

There is Only One Father
by Petra T.

By the time I was born, my dad was already forty-four years old. He had gotten married late because of the war. He had only met my mother, sixteen years his junior, after the war. They fell in love, got married and had two children: my brother, then three and one-half years later, me.

I had a fabulous childhood. For my parents family always came first and we all stuck together. Sometimes we would vacation on a farm; other times we would go to a guesthouse in the mountains or we'd simply stay home and take lovely excursions to places nearby.

Of course, our teenage years were rocky for my parents. I gave them an especially hard time. I ignored curfews and other parental advice and, as a result, I was grounded often. Despite my rebellion, I enjoyed my youth very much and knew full well that my parents' interdictions weren't personal. They really meant well by me.

I had always had a close relationship with my father, in large part because his birthday was the day before mine. He always listened to me and showed a great deal of understanding and caring for whatever I was up to. Because no one else in my family was interested in skiing, my dad was the one who took me to the ski slopes at the tender age of five years old. He would go every Saturday, patiently watching me as I improved my athletic prowess.

After completing my apprenticeship, I had started to earn good money so I decided to move out of the house. I dreamed of having my own apartment, but my dad suffered in the beginning. He kept asking me if I didn't like being at home anymore. Nonetheless, they supported me in my search for an apartment and also helped me look for my first pieces of furniture.

I started a serious relationship so we moved in together. My dad loved my boyfriend like a second son and constantly gave him the feeling that he was a part of the family. With tears in his eyes, my dad walked me down the aisle, saying to my husband, "Take good care of my daughter."

My dad suffered a bit that my brother and I never had kids of our own. He would have loved to have been a grandfather and would have loved and spoiled his grandchildren very much. But fate wouldn't have it. Nevertheless, we had several wonderful godchildren whom we took to visit my parents as often as possible. They treated them as if they were their grandchildren.

Our family loved to celebrate birthdays with great extravagance. Because my dad and I had summer birthdays, we would always plan lovely garden parties for the occasion. On his seventieth birthday, we surprised him with a hot air balloon ride. It was a wonderful celebration!

On his eightieth birthday, I had the idea to give my dad a helicopter ride. We arranged to pick him up at home, take him up for a ride across the Alps and drop him off at the party location we had planned. To this day I still have the image before me as the helicopter landed at our house. My dad clapped his hands with enthusiasm! After the hour-long ride, he didn't want to get out of the helicopter. It was his day, he said. He wanted to continue flying with the pilot.

As his daughter, I realized that my parents wouldn't live forever and that they typically go before we do. I also knew that with every passing birthday, the chances were higher that they would no longer be with us.

My dad was both physically and mentally extremely fit. He would talk with all kinds of people and was interested in all aspects of life. Regarding my own career, he would often ask me how I was doing and showed great interest for my job.

On his eighty-fifth birthday we celebrated his birthday at a nearby restaurant. My husband had been at a tradeshow in Italy, but he returned in time to surprise my father. It made him so happy to have both his sons at his side. He was delighted.

I can vividly remember someone asking my dad on his eightieth birthday if he had plans for his ninetieth. He spontaneously replied: "Let's organize a trip to the moon!" He smiled peacefully. He knew we were good at creating surprises.

For the longest time I had already been planning a moon-themed birthday for his eighty-fifth. I rented a room at a mountain restaurant, called it "Luna Café" and had all the wait staff dress as moon people.

It was 2007. My husband and I had planned a one-week vacation to Italy. Shortly before we left, we visited my parents. My dad was taking his well-deserved nap so my mom asked me to wake him up.

He was sleeping on the couch in my brother's old room. When I opened the door, I was startled. He looked so peaceful. I quickly realized he was breathing quietly so I gently woke him up. It was a Sunday afternoon. We drank coffee on the terrace. We talked about everything under the sun, but my dad seemed listless as if he wasn't really himself. As we got ready to go, I'll never forget his parting words: "Aren't you going to say good-bye?" Although I had just given him a big hug, I got out of the car and hugged him again, saying: "Of course, I'll say good-bye!"

As we drove home, I noticed that my dad had forgotten to wish us a great vacation, which he had always done in the past. Our vacation took place exactly the week we both had our birthdays. Perhaps that was the reason he didn't wish us luck, as if he was unhappy that we couldn't celebrate together, I thought. We planned for my husband to drive to Italy by car so he could attend his trade show and I would come after him via plane.

On that Wednesday after our visit, I called my parents to see how my dad was going. He had been hospitalized just a few months before. Although we had noticed he was a tad unsteady, my mom had buoyed his spirits with her positive energy.

Apparently, my subconscious mind was more preoccupied with the matter than I realized because that night I had the strangest dream that literally woke me up. It was the first time I had ever dreamed of my father's funeral. In my dream I asked myself what I would wear to the occasion. I awoke with a start and couldn't fall back asleep that night.

The next day at work, I got a phone call around lunchtime. Choked with tears, my mother's voice waivered on the other end of the line. She told me that my father was no longer breathing. I told her to call a doctor immediately and then my brother. I ran out of the office and jumped into my car. It didn't feel real, more like being in a movie.

I tearfully called my husband at the tradeshow in Italy and told him what had happened. He begged me not to drive in my current condition, but I couldn't care less. To this day I have no idea how I drove the forty miles without getting into an accident. It started to rain heavily and the autobahn was jammed with traffic. My car started to hydroplane across the lane and the speed limit indicator above the autobahn switched on, telling us to slow down.

Darn it! I thought. I needed to get to my father. I simply couldn't believe he was no longer alive.

While I was still driving, I got a call from my brother confirming the news: our father was dead. How could that be? I prayed to him and called out his name, telling him I wanted to see him and that the rain should stop now. By some miracle, it did indeed stop raining. After slipping and sliding dangerously along the highway at least twice, I finally reached my parents' house.

I stormed into my brother's room. My father was lying on the bed as he had been the Sunday before when I had seen him last. Only this time he didn't open his eyes.

For years I had harbored the fear of what it would be like to lose a loved one. How would I handle the person's death? You can't plan or even think about what you will do in this type of situation. I sat by my dear father's side for about four hours, talking with him, taking him in my arms. I don't really think you know how you will react until you are faced with the situation, but my feeling is you automatically do the right thing.

We lit a candle and opened the window. My mother, brother, his wife and I sat by my father's side and spoke to and about him.

There is never a "right" time to lose a loved one. Age makes no difference. It hurts no matter what and I still miss my father. The best part was that I got to enjoy having a wonderful person by my side for forty-four years. He taught me so much. I am incredibly grateful for that.

My father was forty-four when I was born. Shortly before my forty-fourth birthday and his eighty-eighth, he passed away. The hole he left behind can never been filled. For my mother, who spent over fifty happy years with him, all that is left are memories. We talk about him often and tell stories about him. We may not be able to see him, but we know he is with us always. We find great comfort in that.

For his obituary we chose the following text that says it all: *"His life was love – his love our fortune!"*

A New Horizon
by Rita C.

"I have no talent for fate!" is a ridiculous staying that stems from my "first life" as I ironically call it. The unpredictable and unplanned have always been a horror for me, even as a child. I believed in planning and organization; I liked it when things were orderly and well organized. I placed one hundred percent emphasis on structure in my professional and private life.

As it is in life, such goals take on a life of their own until you know nothing else and can't really accept anything different. For the longest time I carried this attitude that so deeply influenced every aspect of my life's plan: I am considered intelligent, extremely well-structured, results-oriented, studied business administration with a concentration on international marketing, raced up the career ladder of a food cooperation and, in my mid-30s had already taken over international sales within Europe. It meant that I was very successful in sales and was responsible for the licensing of various products in neighboring countries, traveled a lot and carried a weighty responsibility within the company.

A private life? Well, sort of. At the time I had already had an on again off again relationship with a man for a few years whom I really liked, but who continued to push me to the edge with his wish to move in together, get married, have a family, and so on and so forth. No time for that, right? I mean after all I was "only" in my late 30s! My career had absolute priority and if he couldn't accept that, I decided things weren't going to turn out very well for the both of us. Draw the line. Crystal clear. It's better to end in misery then to have endless misery…and all that nonsense.

Just so you know right off the bat not to take me too seriously – luckily, this man didn't either. We have been married for a while now! And as I write these lines, I have to carefully keep my three-year-old daughter's Nutella fingers from touching the computer keyboard because she too "wants to *wite!*" At the same time I have to keep an eye on my two-year-old who is using the remote control of my husband's expensive stereo system as a racecar on the hardwood floor. Vrooommmm! Won't Daddy be surprised when he gets home…

Now then, the crazy turn of events in my life happened like this: I had attended a business meeting for which I had long planned and prepared in Rome where I was to negotiate with the board of a nation-wide delicacy food chain. It was an ambitious plan: If I were successful to license out our most popular items to the Italians, we would have a new very powerful partner in a top sales market. And that would be only the beginning…As I boarded the plane to Rome, I felt like Hannibal, only the other way around and without the elephant: I was crossing the Alps in the opposite direction to conquer Italy.

But the meeting didn't go well. The ladies and gentlemen complained, suddenly saw this, that and the other for the first time, had special questions and wishes, the prices should suddenly be renegotiated, they would only be able to make a decision in a few months at the earliest before making a commitment, not to mention actually going through with the deal. I should do the math again, define new conditions, then I would be allowed back to Rome for another meeting…

The gall they had, asking me to come to Rome under such circumstances at all. And after all that work that I had so perfectly planned and prepared down to the last detail!

I was boiling with anger and frustration, but naturally put on a happy face, leaving the meeting with dignity and a smile on my face, head held high, back straight as an arrow. Outside the building I bummed a cigarette off the doorman even though I had quit smoking a full year before. I hectically banged the keyboard of my Blackberry to see if I could get an earlier flight back to Germany. But my return flight looked like it would be even later because the Italian air traffic controllers suddenly felt the need to strike. Nothing would be moving out of Fiumicino any time soon.

Panicked I jumped into a taxi that took me to the center of Rome to the central train station to take a train back home instead. For once that day I was lucky: There was a night train leaving at 7 p.m. from Rome to Munich, but there were no more sleeping cars left. I didn't care. I bought a bottle of water, got a ticket, entered a compartment in coach class on the train that I had to myself in the beginning and decided to make the most of my confounded situation. The nocturnal journey to Munich would take more than nine hours and although I was exhausted, I was too upset to sleep so I would use my time wisely and work through the night instead.

We pulled out of the station and pretty soon something really odd happened to me. At first the train's movement made me a little sleepy and I started to relax ever so slightly. Somehow I felt as if I were in a movie and I began to almost enjoy the unplanned situation. Hmmm…strange. The laptop sat open on my lap, but I couldn't write anything that made sense. Every now and then I'd type a thing or two into an Excel spreadsheet, but I mostly stared out the window in a dream-like state and fell in love with the landscape that, as we drew closer to Tuscany, became even more enchanting in the twilight. Hmmm….even stranger. What was wrong with me?

At the next stop at 8:15 p.m. in Orvieto, my "splendid isolation" found its end in my train compartment: a young Italian man politely asked, "Permesso?" as he entered the compartment. What could I say to that? So I mumbled, "Si, certo," and demonstratively looked away. But not for long because the young man had brought a scent into the compartment that nearly drove me crazy. Especially for someone who hadn't eaten all day. So I looked at him and saw that this good-looking young guy was carrying a large backpack with him that was apparently the source of those enticing smells.

"Do you speak German?" he asked me now and I nodded: "Please forgive me if it smells like food all of a sudden. Whenever I leave home, my mother and grandmother insist on giving me so much food. Apparently, because they made too much and it would otherwise go to waste, but I know that the day before my departure they start to cook like crazy…They are afraid I might otherwise starve. I'm going to Rosenheim, by the way. I'm studying at the university there. And because I have to disturb you while you are working, I'll just have to share my dinner with you, if I may. Okay?"

Quite honestly, I couldn't resist his beautiful eyes, his broad smile or his charm. And most certainly not the scent of food coming from his backpack. He got started, opening bottle of red wine with no label "from Nonna's vineyard, I even have a few paper cups in my backpack here," a little bowl of tiny, lukewarm *involtini* filled with secret ingredients, a paper plate on which several delicious smelling pizzas were resting beneath a veil of aluminum foil, a glass of pickled artichoke hearts, a linen bag with warm, floury bread with a delicious crust, "Nonna bakes it every day," and finally, a type of large butter jar with a lid which was filled, not with butter, but with a giant piece of tiramisu. I would have committed sin for a dinner like that. Oh, let's be honest: I would have killed for it!

I suddenly lost all interest in my laptop, closing it shut and stuffing it in my briefcase. That's funny, I've always been so disciplined!? What was suddenly wrong with me? Was I willing to throw away all my discipline for a beautiful young Italian man, a couple pieces of pizza and a plastic cup of red wine? Yes, precisely. And it was fabulous!

The Tuscan student from Orvieto was called Marcello. He turned out to be an intelligent young man with whom you could talk about clever and exciting things. He fed me his delicacies relentlessly that his mamma and nonna had made until I was bursting at the seams. I would have loved to travel all the way to Alaska with him. Or better yet: to the ends of the Earth.

We talked and laughed all night long, finished off the last drop of the wine bottle and enjoyed dawn's red light above the Brenner Pass. At some point around 5 a.m., we reached Rosenheim and unfortunately Marcello had to go. When he departed, he looked deeply into my eyes, gave me a tender kiss that tasted mildly like pizza and pressed a note with his cell phone number into my hand. I think he might have just fallen in love with me a bit that night. You know the drill: a young guy and an attractive older woman…

The attractive older woman – that's me – felt incredibly happy and graced with such a gift. The enchanting Marcello, without even knowing it, had changed my life that night: With his casual style and kindness he had made it possible for me to spontaneously react to a situation and a person, a stranger at that! That I could actually relax and chill out.

He taught me that friendliness can change everything. That you could be given not only a lovely meal and wonderful wine, but also warmth, acknowledgement and hospitality. Without a hidden agenda or any other intention other than making someone happy that you happen to meet.

Marcello had made it possible that at 6:30 a.m. that morning when I arrived to Munich, I was the happiest I had been in months if not years. I recognized that all along it was me who had not allowed myself to be spontaneous, relaxed and happy. I will never forget that charming young Italian man.

But I never did call him.

Instead, on that morning at 6:30 a.m., I called my secretary after I decided that the day was too beautiful to waste at work. I left her a voicemail, telling her I had gotten a stomach bug while in Rome…

And then I finally dialed the number of my partner, the man who for years had stood by me with great patience as number two in line behind my work. When he answered, he sounded sleepy, but I spoke anyway: "Good morning. It's Rita. I just took the night train from Rome and I really want to see you. Can I come to you right away? Do you want to play hooky later and take a stroll through the city? I'll even invite you to that Italian place. Oh, before I forget: Please marry me…"

Emergency Call from the Heart

by Mark T.

An audible shrill sound tore through the silence of the room I was in. It permeated the peace and quiet again and again, hovering over me. It was the beeping of the machine onto which I was hooked with multiple sensors.

The device measured my heartbeats, my pulse and my blood pressure, which seemed stable now. I was lucky once again. A few hours before I had been at the movies when a sudden odd feeling overcame me that made me want to rush outside. The pressure in my chest, the fear-inducing breathlessness, the odd blurry vision. The dark room seemed to close in on my tightly like a belt around my body. I first felt unwell, then fearful, then panic-stricken.

The doctor later told me it wasn't a heart attack whose symptoms had scared me, but rather an inflammation of the heart muscle that should be taken seriously. I felt a little safer at the hospital. My blood levels were unambiguous and now I was part of a drama that wasn't being projected onto the screen, but rather had barged into my life. I was in intensive care.

I now know that the final act of my own family drama was the fact that for the past thirty-five years, I was playing a role I didn't even know I had. It wasn't my theater piece in which I played the son. It was my parents' play. For the longest time I would laugh things off, trying to make a comedy out of it and pretending everything was alright. I know today that it was the farthest thing from the truth.

Through my parents' separation and divorce, not only the bond of marriage had been broken, but an enormous crack had run through the entire family. For the longest time I had tried to bridge this gap, but internally it tore me apart. I lost strength, but the same questions kept circling in my head:

Who belongs to whom?

To whom am I allowed to belong?

Am I allowed to love the way I want to or only the way in which people expect me to?

They were questions I didn't ask consciously, but for whose answers I was constantly searching. My heart atrophied in the process, showing me on that day how badly it hurt and could no longer go on this way. I had to take a look. I had never done it before, but now was the time to do it. If I didn't do it now, I would die.

The air smelled clean, but not in a natural way. It had a whiff of chemical sharpness to it. The room was barely lit; in fact only the devices to which I was hooked up cast a little light at all. I have to admit there was that one tiny moment in which I had wished I could die in silence without noticing a thing. It was a wish that death would absolve me of my pain and make my parents' suffering amplify. They should feel what it is like to lose a loved one because that is how I had felt all those years. Thank God that thought didn't float around my head for too long, but in the few seconds it existed, it acted like a drug that carried away all my pain. As the hospital room door opened, every death wish I may have ever had flew right out the window. A lovely older woman in a light blue smock came to my bed to see if I was awake and if everything was alright. Through her presence alone this friendly nurse named Ursula brought such positive vibrations into the room that every negative feeling merely dissolved when she was there.

„Well then, weren't we lucky! So young and you already have heart trouble! You certainly haven't deserved it…" Her words sounded soft and compassionate and her presence felt so familiar, giving me an enormous sense of comfort.

"You know, I may not have deserved it, but I certainly must have worked hard to get into this position," I replied. I spoke with her as if we had known each other all our lives even though we had just met ten minutes before. She was amazing. Her words didn't sound like the phrases of a person who dealt with sick people all day and was trying to be friendly. She said: "When I was your age, my world fell apart, like yours. And even if I don't know you, I know: your new world is going to be magnificent. Trust that it will be so!"

As she spoke with me, she fussed with the instruments and tubes around me, checking that everything was in order. She hummed merrily as she cast me several encouraging looks. After checking the IV, she grasped all five fingers of my left hand with both of her warm hands and said: "My life was exactly as everyone expected it to be. But several years ago I realized only I can determine how my life will be. Follow your heart. It has given you a sign." She looked deep into my eyes, pausing for several seconds. Her gaze was so intense that it numbed the pain in my heart. For the first time in ages, I felt hope again.

It was a feeling no one could or would give me for years, no matter how hard I tried. Suddenly it came from a complete stranger in a place that seemed to be made for hope. The pain lessened. First my spiritual pain, then my physical pain. I now know that my body could have handled even more pain than my heart and my psyche. They were the ones to hit the alarm button. For this level of injury, there isn't a Band-Aid® or doctor in the world that could heal it. The only medicine that can is love. If it goes missing, the heart atrophies. You can't fake it. It is only effective if the love is real. I felt love's strength in that moment. It was filled with sincere compassion from a complete stranger for a suffering person. And that person was me.

I didn't suffer from their separation, but rather from the shadows my parents cast upon me with their mutual hatred. All I wanted was to love them both, but they made it intensely difficult to do so.

A few hours later they both stood before me. For a moment they were united through a common fate that I had created for them. I decided then and there to no longer carry the damage they created through their actions. Instead, I would design my life according to my own dreams. I let the bond go and began my own personal journey. Today I often have a racing heart, but this time it comes from joy and excitement about life itself. I write my own stories and am immensely grateful for everything that I have been allowed to experience.

Train of Thought: From Constriction to Vastness
by Erika S.

January 1945: An ice-cold winter with sub-zero temperatures and endless snowfall. I was just seven years old and was on the run with my mother and sister.

We were fleeing from the Russians! You could hear the constant thundering of cannons as airplanes flew overhead to bomb Berlin. Two Wehrmacht soldiers took us along in their tanker. Our hometown was the city of Wormditt in Eastern Prussia where our aunt ran a pastry shop. All the streets were jammed with fleeing women and children, but the soldiers assured us: "We'll get you out of here!"

Ditches, screaming children and the constant fear of death nestled just beneath our skulls. Originally, we had wanted to take the ship "Wilhelm Gustloff", but the bridge leading up to the ship was blown to pieces. Later the "Wilhelm Gustloff" came under fire and sank with several thousand refugees on board. It could have been us!

Sitting in the tanker now as we fled from the chaos, I suddenly had to go to the bathroom very badly. My mother asked the driver if he would stop briefly so I could relieve myself in the woods. Before I could finish, the truck suddenly took off and I became desperate. To be alone was the worst feeling in the world for me. In that moment, all I thought was *run, run run!*

My mother screamed at the driver to stop because her daughter wasn't back yet. In a full-blown panic I finally reached the truck and was able to climb back in.

Shortly thereafter we continued our journey in a freight car. The cars were packed with about fifty injured soldiers and many families with their belongings.

We never again saw the two soldiers who had picked us up and saved our lives.

When the car doors closed, we sat in complete darkness. We didn't see the light of day during the entire trip Bad Ischl, Austria.

After all the hardship we endured, our mother grew ill. My big sister Eva had to walk the long dangerous path to the emergency pharmacy to get our mother's medicine.

To this day, I can't stand closed doors due to our dramatic escape and the tightness and associated anxiety that came from it. For instance, I can't go to the sauna and always need the doors open.

I also need very large windows around me. I still have nightmares sometimes. I used to scream in my sleep a lot. Ever since our escape I have also suffered from abandonment issues. I have worked through a lot of it on my own. But something good often comes out of something bad.

Years later on a train on the way to school one day a good-looking young man gave me a look. My sister was friends with his brother. He asked me to dance at the school ball. Sparks flew between us. Even my father liked him.

The young man's father ran a well-known construction company in town. After we married, my husband designed our home. He said to me: "You get to have the house you've always wanted!"

We built an "open house" with lots of windows and open spaces. No more constrictions! And this vastness and openness helped me become the free, generous person I am today.

We had two wonderful twin boys who love each other dearly.

A train ride shaped my fate twice in my life: first during the war. The train brought me to safety and away from the horror and fear of death. And then later as a young woman I met the love of my life on a train. He has taught me a lot about the beauty and magnificence of life.

Life's journey is one of constant movement. Hop on that train and watch as something new unfolds!

My American Dream
by Franz W.

I grew up in a middle-class family. My sister is four years older than I am and in my life, sports has always played a huge role. With his Italian roots, my father always pushed me to perform at my very best. I even won a few trophies in skiing. My father saw me as a famous ski racer, but to be honest, getting up early on the weekends and going to all those competitions started to get on my last nerve.

During my studies in economics, I got the chance to intern in New York at a German film company. During that time, I fed my internal desire for independency and freedom. "The Big Apple" and me! Girls, beer and cool people. What else could a young man want? It was the best time of my life.

Upon my return, my yearning for America grew. After my internship, the company offered me a job in Munich as a camera sales representative for Bavaria. I was responsible for the international markets and covered the US, Canada, England, New Zealand and Australia.

I then got the chance again to return to New York in their training program. Upon my return to Munich I was promoted as the assistant to the technical senior management. My career was very promising. A competing firm offered me a job that I found most enticing. They wanted to send me to the US!

My uncle who ran the family business checked out the company and found it had major financial issues. Instead, he offered me a job at his company. Our family owns a delicacy shop. I would be responsible for restructuring, marketing and personnel. They were planning to completely relaunch the company and I would be responsible for the commercial business in the East.

I had worked for my uncle's company for four years when my former boss from the film industry walked by me one day and called out: "Call me!" We arranged a time to meet a month later. He offered me a job in the US. It just so happened that I had booked a flight to New York for some vacation so I was able to meet with the head of the American branch while I was there. The meeting occurred in February of 1994. Five months later I moved to America.

In the US I earned exactly half what I had in Germany, but that didn't matter. I was getting closer to my American dream. My chance meeting with my old boss and his encouragement to "call me!" changed my life completely.

I have lived and worked in the US for over twenty years since that time. Seventeen of those years I was in New York, five in Los Angeles. The best part was that my high school sweetheart from

Germany met me after her girlfriend pushed her to do so. Today she is my wife and lives with me in Los Angeles!

We are both extremely happy that we left our "comfort zone" to let our dreams come true.

It was the moment that changed my life forever!

I was "the loser"
by Linus R.

I am turning eighteen soon and will graduate high school next year. So far so good. But I have to admit I've had a few really bad experiences that make me wonder how I survived them without serious damage to my soul. When I was younger, I was bullied so severely for an entire year at school that I felt I had no way out.

Up to the end of primary school, everything had been fine. I had really good grades, friends in the neighborhood, attended an after-school program, played soccer with my friends after doing homework or we were out and about on our bikes in our quarter. My mama is single and works. We love each other dearly and she was glad that we managed our day-to-day lives so well. It wasn't until I was about to switch to secondary school after the fourth grade that things took a turn for the worse. My mama made a bad decision, even if she meant well at the time.

The secondary school in our quarter, to which a few of my primary school friends would be going, didn't offer an after-school program. Because she didn't come from work until 4 p.m., she looked for a school with a full-time program that was situated in a different city quarter. I would take the school bus in the mornings and be brought back around 4 p,m. in the afternoons. I begged her to let me go to the secondary school nearby. I promised I would make my own lunch and do my homework on my own. But nothing seemed to help. She thought I was too young. At the age of eleven, I switched to the new school in September of that year.

I have to say I was a totally normal boy. I still am. I looked rather normal, wasn't particularly good-looking, but not weird-looking either. I get along with people in general and always had friends and buddies. I was good in school, but not a super-student or anything. No brown-noser with extraordinary abilities, except perhaps in sports. I got along with the teachers pretty much too. I wore normal clothing and talked with the others. But from the very first day in the new school, I began to question if I really was okay or if there was something wrong with me.

The students in my class all came from different parts of the city. They all took the bus home in the afternoons. No one really knew each other, but you could see that after one or two days, cliques were starting to form. Boys made friends with those who had similar interests and would hang out at recess in the schoolyard. The seating arrangement was solidified. I sat next to a kid on the same bench, but he didn't talk to me from day one. And when I tried to join a clique during recess and followed behind one of them in the courtyard, one of them was guaranteed to turn around and say: "Get lost, you loser." And if I approached a group that was kicking around a ball, one of them would immediately say: "Get out of here, you don't get to play with us."

I was completely at wit's end. I didn't understand it, but somehow had to accept it. What else could I do? After just a few weeks I was so isolated and "invisible" to the other students that various teachers took notice and tried to intervene. They took special care of me and tried to mediate between me and my classmates by building extra working groups during class or sports teams in the schoolyard to include me or even groups of two during afternoon instruction. But none of it helped. Only when it was unavoidable or a teacher was standing nearby did one of my classmates even say a word to me. Other than that, nada.

At home I also fell out of touch with my former school friends and buddies. When I finally got home in the late afternoon, we could no longer meet. We were all only ten or eleven years old and couldn't be outdoors after dark. And on weekends most of them were out and about with family.

I hid my pain from my mother for quite some time. She noticed in the evenings that I had somehow gotten quieter, but when she asked me what was wrong or how things were going in school, I usually just said: "Fine." She'd grin and say: "Getting anything out of you boys is like pulling teeth!"

It was only after my grades went downhill toward the end of the first school year because I couldn't sleep well at night or concentrate during the day and when I had lost all desire to prepare for the next day's classes that my mother became gravely concerned and made an appointment with my teacher.

Quite honestly at that point after a year of isolation in school, I had started to think about a way out in the way an eleven-year-old would think: run away, live on the street, emigrate to America, work as a cabin boy, join the circus, dumb stuff like that. Anything but going to school every morning!

Our teacher told my mother then that I had "massive issues with my classmates" during class, lunch and in the after-school program. What bullshit! I didn't have a problem with the others; they had a problem with me! But that wasn't the point. My mother was shocked and sat me down that very evening. At first I didn't want to tell her anything because I thought the whole time that it had been my fault that I no longer had friends. Something must be wrong with me because no one wanted anything to do with me. It wasn't that easy to admit as a little kid or to even formulate it in a way that an adult could understand.

This time my mother made the right decision. Thank God! She thought I should finish the school year there and suggested that I find a way to finish out the last few weeks. We would then have summer vacation and in the new school year she would have me switch schools back to my quarter where a lot of my old primary school friends attended school. The very next day we made an appointment with the school principal, explaining the emergency situation and arranging for my move the following school year.

Then she gathered her courage to call the mother of my old buddy Paul to shyly ask if she might allow me to accompany Paul after school to eat lunch and spent the afternoon doing homework at his house under her supervision. She offered to pay Paul's mother who was most willing to help out until my mom came home from work.

Now that I am nearly an adult, I can image how hard it must have been for my mom to swallow her pride and ask a stranger for help. Not to mention the money that we barely had to pay for it. But my mom did the right thing and I am ever so grateful to this day that she did.

Knowing that I would soon leave, I was able to spend the last few weeks in my old school with relative ease. I tried not to make anything out of the other classmates' mean behavior. I perked up immensely now that the burden had been lifted from my shoulders.

During summer vacation I spent the whole time with my old buddies. It felt as if we had never parted. And I *almost* – and I really mean *almost* – was excited about my first day of school in the new school. Like a young child who is excited about the next school year. Nonetheless, I have to admit I was scared stiff the first day of sixth grade. After all, it was a totally new school. I didn't just have my old primary school buddies around me, but also a bunch of new classmates that I should get to know as well. And new teachers too. I didn't sleep well the night before the first day of school.

It was only after the first recess bell that I could breathe more easily. I walked stiffly from one place to the next, awkwardly grabbing my snack and drink out of my bag when someone from behind slapped me on my shoulder and yelled: "Hey, slowpoke!"

As I turned around in surprise, I saw a funny face with a bunch of freckles and a cheeky grin. It was my new classmate Michael. Four or five other grinning boys stood behind him. I had noticed them earlier that morning because they were loud and boisterous. "Man, Linus, make it snappy. We want to toss the ball during recess. Do you want to join us?"

That very moment not only saved my first day of school, relieving one of my biggest concerns of all times, but in the end it changed my entire life. In one fell swoop I recognized that I didn't have to "be" something special, didn't have to "perform", say something clever or be cool to be accepted. I had value and was worth being liked!

I will never forget that cheeky Michael and his other buddies. We are friends to this day and have started making plans after graduation to go to the same college and live in the same pad...

An Experience That Turned Everything on its Head

by Hans F.

It was the year 1999 and we were doing extremely well. My wife Erika and I had simply everything our hearts desired. We had a great marriage, lived in a beautiful home and were both active in the real estate and construction business. Over a period of thirty years we had built a substantial business with up to 45 employees. Our extraordinary success gave us cause to believe every day anew that we were doing the right things.

From the outside looking in, we had no reason to change anything. We were both more than satisfied and yet from one moment to the next, we threw in the towel in order to take our professional and personal lives in a completely new direction. But I'm getting ahead of myself. Let's start this odd story from the very beginning.

Erika, who as the owner of a successful real estate company was "tied in" very well businesswise, suffered from severe neck strain and tension. It was rather typical for someone who works at a desk all day, we thought, and searched out all kinds of medical advice from doctors and physical therapists. But her attacks worsened by the day while her diagnoses grew more vague. They couldn't pinpoint any physical causes for her pain and therefore boiled it down to "continuous stress" and "too much screen time" at work. Erika's painful odyssey took two years without even the slightest improvement in sight.

That is, until the day one of her female employees gave her a tip to consult her naturopath. Wolfgang Paliga applied an unusual method for examining patients: He tested them with a divining rod. We later found out the method was called radiesthesia. The naturopath's immediate diagnosis claimed: "You have a problem with your upper cervical spine along with an additional toxins and vaccination stress. Furthermore, you are sleeping on a water vein in your upper cervical spine that has been turning for two years."

Genius or charlatan?

At first we were speechless and didn't know if we could believe such "humbug". "He's crazy," was my first reaction. We have been living in the same house for seventeen years. How could a water vein suddenly enter our bedroom? But the pain was stronger than the doubt and Erika suddenly remembered that we had moved our bed exactly two years ago. So she agreed to the strange treatment. After draining the toxins, the naturopath adjusted her neck and suggested we definitely move the bed to another part of the room. As an alternative, he showed us a small stainless steel tube that was apparently able to "eradicate" the pathogenic effect of the water vein. The entire house would thereby be neutralized through this method and free from geopathogenic radiation and electrosmog. We decided to do just that. We got ourselves the device – a so-called *memonizer* – and my wife was instantly pain-free! That was the moment that completely unhinged our thinking and later our actions.

The point of no return…

We truly couldn't believe it, but the effect was so overwhelming that we began to delve deeper into the topic. We had specialized in ecological construction in the real estate business, but this here was a completely different dimension. I had a lot of discussions with the naturopath who impressively demonstrated the effect that a chip can have to protect you from electrosmog while travelling. I was so excited that I contacted the chip's developer, Mr. Winfried M. Dochow.

His way of thinking was completely new terrain for me. He introduced me to a holistic world that had lain hidden for Erika and me up to now. With great enthusiasm I grew more and more familiar with the material during the course of the year and accompanied Mr. Dochow to events and client meetings during which time I became more and more convinced about the astonishing effects his devices had.

Somewhere along the line I reached the point of no return. Erika and I were on fire about these products and we wanted for other people to regain their health with the help of these devices and to discover the energetic connections that holistic healing has.

Of course, it was also in Winfried M. Dochow's interest as he was more of a developer and less of a salesman. He had too little time to dedicate to marketing and distributing the *memonizer*.

After an incredibly moving year that had placed my thinking and my view of the world on its head, I decided to give up my successful construction business and to start all over again. A decision that had far-reaching consequences and that had to be planned down to the last detail. After all, I carried a great deal of responsibility for several flourishing businesses and – most importantly, for a large number of engaged employees. At the same time, I had a burning desire to dedicate all my time to *memon* – the name we chose for our new company – so that more and more people could benefit from this technology.

It was a life dream that not many in my immediate vicinity really shared. Erika needed some time before she could dedicate herself to *memon*. She first needed to find a trustworthy successor to whom she could hand over her real estate business and her employees with a good conscience.

Oh to dedicate one's all to something!

Erika and I never regretted having taken the leap of faith to do so. But what seemed so natural to us wasn't shared by the people around us. The more harmless versions of their opinions: "You're nuts! Totally insane, completely naïve!" We offered our employees the chance to follow our vision, but only four of them found the courage to trade a financially sound position for one in a start-up company.

Our move from the material world to the etheric world wasn't always a bed of roses. After openly making such a drastic change, we had to allow it to permeate every area of our lives. Our unconventional decision not only placed our professional lives on their heads, but also our social ones too. It was a very turbulent and instructive time, but we are still happy about our courageous decision and perseverance to stand by our convictions. Today it is crystal clear that we had finally found our life's truest purpose through the decision we made.

We see how right our decision was by the great enthusiasm with which people who are able to be open to holistic methods have when they first realize the level of basic healing that is possible on the subtlest of levels. Today, a full fifteen years after our "personal change," society has changed dramatically. More and more people are conscious that they need to take good care of themselves and their energetic surroundings. They are much more open to the things between heaven and Earth that we may not be able to see, but that have an enormous influence on us.

Just like Erika and myself, numerous clients and partners are extremely grateful for the *memon* technology and the holistic form of well-being it brings along with it.

Never Say Never...
by Theresa V.

"Get married? Not in a million years!" As a teenager I used to drive my parents crazy by saying that, but they didn't really take me seriously. It will take care of itself once the child finds Mr. Right, they thought. "The child" had other plans, however, that involved a man or better yet several, but my life's motto was clear and defined: "I always want to be free and independent."

To be honest I have no idea where my aversion toward commitment, marriage and family comes from. My parents were a death-do-us part kind of couple, married for more than sixty years and pretty happy with one another. I really liked my parents and siblings and enjoyed attending every family event I could. I loved my nieces and nephews and appreciated my heritage.

I have a rather relaxed attitude toward men. I think it comes from the fact that I simply don't understand men and that I also don't take them all that seriously. I simply like men. End of story. And as things tend to go, I experienced my first big love in my youth that ended dramatically and tearfully after a few years. His fault. Not mine. Several other love relationships followed, some intense, others more superficial, sometimes I ended it, sometimes he did.

During college I enjoyed my life immensely. Back then you could spend a few extra semesters figuring things out without being penalized in any way and you were still able to get a halfway decent job. I had had a couple nice relationships, but took great pains to ensure none of these young men got any serious ideas. And the expression "young men" gets to the crux of the matter: I never preferred older men. Even men my age made me yawn with boredom. I found them suburban, established, etc.

I was the young superwoman and wanted to stay that way. I was considered the most satisfied, happiest single around with a lovely two-room apartment, a tiny car, beautiful clothes, a large circle of friends and the best girlfriends ever.

On a professional level I also had a good start after college. I had gotten a University assistant position that was limited to two years. But everyone around me assured me that with my talent, credentials and abilities I would certainly get a really good job afterward.

There was a company in my hometown that was my absolute dream employer. I decided to blindly apply to any position they might have available. To cut a long story short: I got one of the most desirable positions in the entire company. With the understanding that lots of expectations and demands would be placed one me to perform at a consistently high level and that I would have to deal with a loose cannon for a boss. But I was certain I could handle it. From the very day I received the acceptance letter I was determined to do everything in my power to stay as long as possible in this wonderful company and to build up something really good for myself. As of now, that was my top priority.

The company had a very good work environment. A lot of the departments celebrated and the head of the company would pay for a round of drinks for all employees whenever the company had something to celebrate. I started my job in February at the tail end of Carnival. And it so happened that our top executive allowed us time off on Fat Tuesday as of noon. We rocked the house in the company that day, including a little hanky-panky amongst some of the employees. As the newest and very attractive colleague, I received a lot of advances myself, all of which I kindly, but firmly refused.

There was a very good-looking colleague in the company who was most charming and collegial. He was the heartthrob of every lady in town. His grand reputation as a heartbreaker went well beyond our company and extended to the entire industry…Luckily I had little to do with this particular co-worker because we worked in separate departments and we had no overlap in the production process. That's why it was particularly noticeable – and it wasn't just me who noticed, but also other co-workers of mine – that he "happened" to be in my proximity a lot. It got on my last nerve because I didn't want to start anything with someone in the company or to risk any gossip from leaking out. Besides he really wasn't my type, was thirteen years older than me and, to top it all off, in a relationship. In terms of the company hierarchy, he stood two rungs above me.

Carnival was over, daily life resumed and I punished my co-worker by ignoring him completely without being impolite. But I sent very clear signals: No, thank you.

In May the large annual executive conference was called and our department got busy preparing and putting on a seamless event for the company. We organized space, catering, equipment, public relations, etc. The department head was invited to attend the large, fancy dinner with the executive board and because I had really rocked it out for the company and had done a superior job, he invited me to accompany him.

I oscillated between enthusiasm, anticipation and nervousness. Bought a fancy dress, went to the hair salon. I caught myself cleaning up my apartment on the morning of the event before going to work. As if struck by lightning, I realized that I was going to take home that good-looking co-worker tonight! I turned hot, then cold, then nauseous. I am a pretty intuitive person. Even as a child, I had "odd" insights and thoughts and trusted that everything had a reason. This time I didn't feel quite right about it and I prayed that it was all just nonsense.

For the rest of the day, I was a nervous wreck. I desperately tried to suppress thoughts about how the evening would end and told myself that I must have been wrong. Luckily, my co-worker sat quite far away from me at a different table. I didn't look over to him and avoided any kind of eye contact whatsoever. I drank mineral water because I didn't trust myself to drink wine. I wanted to remain in absolute control of the evening.

During the final course of the meal the seating arrangement loosened and people started taking their dessert plates to other tables to chat with other colleagues. People drank a lot. One female colleague from Controlling had obviously intended on snatching the attractive co-worker. She fought her way to the seat next to him. As I happened to look in his direction, I saw how she had placed her arm around his neck and the other hand on his thigh. And then like a shot of lightning, the thought raced through my mind: Don't even try it, chickadee. The guy is coming home with *me* tonight. And later he's going to be my husband.

I nearly fell from my chair and decided it was time to go home right away. Alone!!!

As I stood at the coat rack to get my coat, he was suddenly standing behind me and said; "You can't just leave. I've been thinking about you all day and I am coming with you." I was speechless. We went together to the taxi stand, then drove to my apartment in complete silence as if we had reached a silent agreement. It was only when we arrived that I accepted my reality. We fell into each other's arms and haven't spent a day apart since.

Next year the love of my life and I will celebrate our thirtieth wedding anniversary!

Barbara's Healing Story
by Barbara R.

I feel like an ordinary person most of the time, but I've been given an amazing gift that I don't deserve, and that makes me feel like I'm somebody important. I'm 56 years old now, and my life is wonderful. I was born in America, I have four siblings, and my mother is still alive and well. I completed high school and three years of college, and I've had various jobs over the years and met some great people. I married a wonderful man at the age of 27. I have three beautiful girls, two of which are now married, and one perfect grandson. I get to travel on occasion which is such a perk! But let me tell you something that interrupted my life as early as age 20 (which was 1980).

I was diagnosed with Multiple Sclerosis in 1992. I actually had MS for years but didn't know it was the cause of all the symptoms I had been dealing with. I had gone to a neurologist who did an MRI (magnetic resonance imaging) on my brain. When the doctor called me and gave me this diagnosis I just remember being stunned but not truly able to understand what it meant.

Multiple sclerosis (MS) is an unpredictable, often disabling disease of the central nervous system that disrupts the flow of information within the brain, and between the brain and body. In multiple sclerosis, damage to the myelin in the central nervous system — and to the nerve fibers themselves — interferes with the transmission of nerve signals between the brain and spinal cord and other parts of the body.

Every person who has this disease may deal with completely different symptoms depending on what area of myelin tissue is being attacked. Some of the common symptoms of MS include fatigue, mood changes, difficulties with attention, learning, and memory, muscle rigidity or stiffness, weakness or poor coordination, numbness and tingling, pain in arms and legs, visual disturbances, and sometimes bladder and bowel problems.

While I was attending college, I went to the university hospital for all my medical needs. I received very good care by a number of medical professionals. When I explained my numb and tingling sensations to them, they had me receive a CAT scan (an X-ray image made using computerized axial tomography). Then the doctor did a pin-prick test on my feet, asking me if the pain I felt was sharp or dull. All of this was inconclusive. I overheard the doctor say to a technician in the room that it might be multiple sclerosis. I never returned to that doctor, thinking, 'yea, right!'

I remember experiencing a numb and tingling sensation in my feet when I was newly married in the late 1980's. The company I worked for was participating in a parade and my husband had helped work on the company float. About half way through the parade my feet were numb and tingly and causing me pain, too. I got rid of my favorite tennis shoes thinking that they were the culprit of my pain. I experienced pain in my legs off and on for years. We found a topical pain relief 'daily treatment for chronic everyday pain' which was veterinarian recommended for horses. This lotion would begin working after putting a damp washcloth on it and 'wow' the heat! It did relieve the pain for a while. The next few years, my sweet husband would rub my legs and feet whenever I asked to ease the pain.

In the early 90's, I also dealt with overwhelming fatigue and weakness in my limbs, making it unsafe to drive. My arms were so weak and shaky, on occasion I couldn't even write or carry the baby. The symptoms would start slowly and become worse until they stabilized for a few weeks then slowly dissapaited. Each time it was completely random as to which part of my body would be affected and totally uncontrollable.

I read and became more knowledgeable about the latest 'cures' and treatments. The research at that time was in the experimental stages and nothing really helped. I remember reading about honey bee stings being an antidote. Yikes!

I realized I really needed help. My husband was in the military and sometimes he would be deployed for undetermined amounts of time. When the doctor called with the diagnosis, my husband and I had a beautiful three year old and a precious newborn baby. The challenges were very real and quite debilitating. Just living a normal daily routine was extremely challenging.

After coming to the end of myself, I realized that I believe in a powerful God so I decided to ask for prayer. When I approached my pastor, he told me that he would call me sometime soon. I didn't understand this response but I knew it was okay, so I asked all my family and husband (he was deployed at the time) to pray during this time also. They did. They fasted and prayed. The pastor called me in two weeks (I'm sure now that they were fasting and preparing, too) and said that he and 7 of the deacons along with his wife (who watched my girls for me) would come to my house to pray for me.

It was a Wednesday evening after church and they came, anointed me with a dab of oil on my forehead and prayed for God to heal me. They prayed in the name of His Son Jesus Christ and claimed the promise of healing represented in the blood that He shed for us on the cross. I didn't feel anything special at that moment, but I hugged and thanked them all and said goodbye.

After they had all gone, I realized that ALL my symptoms were gone!! I remember dancing all over the house with my 3 year old and lighting every candle in the house! I was having a praise party!! I called my husband and told him. He was ecstatic along with me! It was late or I would have called EVERYONE right then!!!

I have not had any MS symptoms in 24 years even though I have had another MRI that shows the lesions (sclerosis) are still there.

I had another baby girl three years after my healing and all my girls are grown and doing very well. We are SO blessed! I try to celebrate my life and mobility often! I don't want to take it for granted. I could have easily been wheelchair bound, or worse, but I'm not!!

God is so good!

How One Decision Changes Everything
by Greg J.

I regularly attend seminars to learn new ideas and paradigms that I can use to improve myself overall. One such event was held over several consecutive days in Santa Barbara, California, where I live. There were about a hundred of us in the class. The facilitators put us into pairs and led us through a series of questions and some interesting exercises.

Being open to new processes, both Rocky and I were committed to doing all the exercises without prejudging. Even though some of the exercises felt unnecessarily uncomfortable to me, I still participated fully.

On the second night of the seminar, our homework was to fill in the blank in this phrase: "Life is _____." To me, this was easy, because at this point in my life, things matter. Every minute matters and I'm purposefully, crafting, designing, and really living life happily every single day. Now, I know that living with purpose probably isn't the normal way most people live, but I thought my answer to this question about what life is couldn't be too far off normal, right?

Morning came. Since I believe that with a new seat in the classroom comes a new perspective, I sat in a different seat, in the center of the back row. The facilitator asked for the hands of the people who'd done their homework and nearly everyone raised their hand. He said, "So let me ask you, what is life? I'd like to hear your answers."

My hand shot up with about 20 others and he started calling on people.

"Pain!" someone yelled out.

"Disappointment," said the next girl.

Then he pointed to me. I yelled, "Life is freaking awesome!" I meant it—I wasn't trying to be the funny guy. It was totally heartfelt and genuine.

The facilitator's response was, "Too broad." And he moved on.

A woman in her forties added, "Life is heartbreak." A teenager mumbled, "Sadness." The next person said, "Waiting to die."

Wait, what? Hold on here… Life is waiting to die? Who are the people in this room? Are all these people (who are clearly hurting inside) an accurate representation of how the average population of the world feels?

My heart sank. I was feeling grateful and lucky for how amazing my life is in every area with so many people around me in sadness. I didn't realize the pain most people are living in—not at all.

The facilitator said with a big smile, "Nope, you're all wrong. Life is dangerous." Then, in case we didn't hear it the first time, he repeated, "Life is dangerous." He told us we are all afraid—scared of the people sitting next to us, in front of us, at work, at school, the people on the streets, the people we don't know—everywhere in the world, all of them. We're frightened of them and they're frightened of us.

For some reason, the word "dangerous" wasn't too broad of a concept, but "awesome" was clearly over the top.

At this point I was thinking, *This is complete nonsense!* I turned to the girl next to me, who was in her mid-20s, and said, "I want you to know that I'm not scared of you, and I hope you aren't frightened of me, because I'm not a scary guy and this world is an amazing, beautiful place and is rarely dangerous." She smiled and assured me that she was definitely not afraid of me.

That session illustrates one of the most important lessons I've learned about happiness:

It Is Exactly What You Think It Is

Whatever dominates your thoughts: that is how you live your life. In other words, you get whatever you focus on with intensity for prolonged periods of time. This works all the time, every time, good and bad, for everyone. You say that life is dangerous? You'll see danger everywhere. You say that life is heartbreak? Even in your best relationships, you'll be looking ahead to the moment that it will all come to a tragic, bitter end rather than expecting and enjoying the best that already is.

Have you ever known people who are "victims"? They expect bad things to happen, and they do. Bad luck seems to follow them around. If you listen to these people, they ask themselves questions like, "Why do bad things always happen to me? What terrible thing is going to happen next? Why can't I catch a break?"

You get what you focus on, and you also get the answers to the questions that you ask. What do you think would happen if "victims" asked themselves questions that they might actually want the answers to—like, "How **can** I make this happen? What if things worked out perfectly, what would that look and feel like?"

If you are consumed by the thought of terrible things happening, they will continue to happen. If you want to change what happens to you, it starts by changing how you think. And if you want to be happy, you have to learn how to think differently.

You need to think like happy people think.

It's My Life!
by Roger Z.

I have just gotten home from work, jump into the shower and am mentally already in front of the television watching the Olympic games. It doesn't sound that special and most likely a lot of people felt that way during the time in Rio. But there is one thing that sets me apart from most everyone else: I wanted to be there too and should have been with the other athletes to experience the famous "Olympic spirit" and the adrenaline that races through your body when the start signal goes off.

I was eleven years old when I started to dedicate every part of my being to triathlons. Sports have always been the most important thing in my life, but the triathlon was supposed to be something extra special for me. I was extremely passionate, trained daily, wanted to get better and better so that one day I could fulfill my greatest dream: Olympia. As one of the best in my age group, I was soon no longer just dreaming about the Olympic games. It was starting to become a reality as the chance to participate became much more likely.

I would often get up well before school to train and to improve my times bit for bit. Proud as punch I would often return from championships with a medal. All those years I was able to rely on the immense support from my family. That is, until alleged neck tension changed everything, placing me before the hardest thing I had ever had to face in my life.

It was the winter of 2002. I was sixteen years old and had just spent a normal day training. I went to bed early because I had to go to school the next day. When I awoke, I noticed intense tension running down my neck. I called the club's physiotherapist right away because I thought the pain must be coming from muscle tension. After the physical therapist had treated me, I skipped school and went back to bed.

When I wanted to get up around midday, I had a high fever and noticed that the skin all over my body had turned yellow. My general practitioner sent me to the nearest hospital, but the exam there gave us no clear diagnosis. My mother tells me now that the doctor had come to her back then, shaking his head and saying he had never seen such bad blood levels in his entire career.

When I was released back home, it took exactly one day and one night before it was clear my symptoms were more serious than we had originally thought. My fever shot up to 105.8°F, my entire body turned color again only this time it looked like blue flecks speckled across my skin. Back to the hospital I went, but no one really knew what to do. Several doctors were consulted. It was only after I fell into a comatose state that night that the attending physician decided to give me a spinal tap. He discovered I had meningitis that had strongly attacked my body due to the delay in treatment. After they placed me in an artificial coma, I have virtually no memory of what happened next…

At the time my parents were in a state of emergency. They sat by my bedside every day, hoping that my condition would get better. For days on end they could barely detect any kind of reaction to the treatment. Both my blood pressure and pulse remain unchanged and my reflexes showed no response. A nurse suggested that my parents try familiar music. They sat next to my bed and played one song after the other, songs that had accompanied me in my earlier life or that I simply loved to hear. Finally, when they played Bon Jovi's "It's My Life", I showed a reaction: my blood pressure and pulse started to rise.

I only know about these events through my parents' stories. Back then they were extremely worried that I may never wake up again. I will never forget the first thing I remembered after waking up from my coma: It was my coach's red sweater that he wore when he sat at my bedside. It is odd, really, that out of such a dramatic situation something as banal as a red sweater is what you remember most.

Thereafter I spent several more weeks in intensive care, fighting against epileptic fits. My whole life was suddenly about taking medications. But the whole time I was obsessed with one thought: how fast could I return to sports?

At the time no one told me I would never reach the level of performance I used to have ever again and that my dream of Olympia would have to fade.

Again and again I tried to fight my way back to the top. I trained daily, but I have to admit that the ensuing headaches after training were torturous. I was devastated, but every time I would reach one little milestone of success, it would spark a glimmer of hope in me.

I tortured myself for six months without any visible progress until I finally reached the point that I had to admit that it was over. My dreams had been destroyed, my greatest goal in life erased. At the time I had no idea what I should do next. I soon realized however that I would always love sports even if I had to take on a different role in it.

Early on it became clear that the only other thing besides active sports that I wanted to do would be to become a physical therapist. And that's what I did. It was a step of which I am very proud even to this day! Even if my illness rocked my world at the time, I was able to rebuild my existence piece by piece, changing only a few bits to rearrange the puzzle of my life. In the end, the puzzle was once again complete.

Today I have my own practice and work together with a great team. A lot of athletes walk through my door and with them blows the wind of the Olympic spirit, showing me that I can still be involved, perhaps in a different way than I had intended, but that I am still a part of a greater whole just the same.

Our Engine Stopped!
by Julia K.

My husband and I have a very cool experimental airplane! We love to fly places even if it's just for lunch or a short visit with family or friends. After a lot of thought and planning we decided to take an excursion with friends but let me explain…

My husband is a brilliant man and I'm continually amazed by his multiple talents and constant drive to create things. When he's not at work he stays busy with various hobbies. If he's not busy, he goes stir crazy.

One of his fabulous creations is an airplane. Yes, that's right, a real airplane that actually flys. It took him about 17 years to build it because it was a hobby and he didn't let it consume him or take quality time away from family, so he took his time and slowly but surely built it from scratch. He did buy the engine and propeller but he built the airplane from plans out of foam, fiberglass, wires, hoses, tubes… you get the idea. There were so many decisions when it was just an idea but he finally came up with the airplane plans that satisfied his hankering. The decision was made to build the ERacer experimental aircraft. It has a canard wing in the front of the plane and the engine is in the back.

His degree out of college was in geology but after the oil crisis in the late '80s, he decided to pursue his fascination with flying. He signed up with the Air Force and after 20 years, retired. He's been flying for a major airline now since 2008 so he is a very good pilot with thousands of flying hours and extensive experience in different aircraft.

We have flown together on occasion but he loves to go fly alone quite often. His ERacer airplane had been proven time and time again.

We were excited to find a group of home-builders (airplane builders) with the same type of aircraft as we had. They flew together to the Bahamas every year for a week. We decided we were going to join them! All of us would meet in Florida, spend the night, and leave the next day from there.

The flight to Florida was uneventful and we were happy to meet these new friends with similar interests. The next day, the person in charge determined the groups of airplanes that would fly together to the Bahamas. Out of 7 airplanes, we would be flying fourth in the first flight of four. Then a flight of three would follow after us. After briefing the variables, we started engines together and taxied out to the runway. The three planes in front of us took off beautifully and it was our turn. We pulled onto the runway, ran the engine up and started the takeoff roll. The takeoff was uneventful and we climbed up to join the other airplanes ahead of us. When we were about 500 feet in the air our engine stopped! I felt a slight sinking feeling and I immediately began praying as my husband began trying to figure out what went wrong and restart the engine. He then started to look for a suitable place to try to set the airplane down in one piece. I remember him turning quickly toward me and saying, 'You need to keep praying.'

I was a little stunned at this statement because I WAS praying but this verified that we were indeed in a precarious situation that could go bad quickly. I don't think I had time to think very much about family, friends, my last will and testament, etc. I just prayed! I prayed that God's angels would hold our wings up and set us down somewhere safely.

My husband saw a large highway and since it was a Sunday morning, traffic was not bad. Getting back to the runway would *definitely* be optimal in our choices of places to set down but if he couldn't turn back then he could land on the highway, *IF* the engine *didn't* restart. The engine did restart for two short bursts, perhaps a few seconds each, but then shut off again. It was just enough to turn the plane back toward the airfield. As we dropped out of the sky he was able to nervously request a crossing runway for an emergency landing. There was an aircraft on the runway whose pilot overheard what was going on and quickly got off the runway for our unexpected return.

I remembered seeing the grass off the end of the runway getting closer and closer very quickly and then reaching the edge of the asphalt right before we belly landed the plane. We slid out of control like a ride at an amusement park propelled forward, veering right, then left for a few hundred feet until we finally stopped. Knowing we needed to exit the plane as quickly as possible in case of fire, we popped the canopy and got out. No fire, thankfully.

We called our family to report our traumatic event and made sure everyone knew we were alright. I even had my husband take a picture of me sitting on the wing in the middle of the runway saying that, after all, this *was* our vacation.

We left some paint and fiberglass scrapings on that runway but since there were no injuries, we moved the airplane to some tie-downs on the tarmac and the FAA took down all the information. This took hours but eventually we decided to continue on to the Bahamas the next day via commercial airline. Why waste our vacation plans at an airport in Florida. Our new friends were delighted when we arrived in the Bahamas the next day and greeted us as if we were family! They found it hard to believe that we had come anyway!!

They all wanted to know the specifics of our potential demise and help figure out the problem since they are all builders and this could have been any one of us. We had a wonderful time with these kind people and swapped many stories.

I will admit, many things go through your mind during and after an incident like this. You tend to reevaluate your life and your relationships. We felt that we had been given a great opportunity to live our lives with a new perspective.

We now know to be prepared at all times to meet our Creator because one never knows when that time may be. We've always loved spending time with family but it seems more special now. We make sure all our relationships are healthy. We know that forgiveness is the best and greatest option to any offense. We love to smile often and let people know how important they are to us. And we KNOW to keep on praying even when our lives *aren't* flashing before our eyes.

After our vacation, my husband travelled back to Florida and fixed the airplane, good as new. He built it, so he obviously he could fix it. The culprit was a new air filter that had weakened and had been sucked into the manifold. He put an appropriate air filter back on and it's been working perfectly ever since. It didn't really take more than a couple of days and the airplane was home again, tucked away in the hanger. We've even gone back to the Bahamas in our plane with our new friends since then!

My Second Life
by Gerry W.

It was shortly after my fiftieth birthday. I was relaxing in the garden with a beer in my hand, listening to beautiful music through my earphones and loving my life. How happy I am, I thought. Everything is so harmonious.

For the past twenty years I had been a most successful external sales rep for a leading food cooperation. I was married, had two great sons and a lovely dog. My boys love soccer and as their father, I often attend their games. As mentor and coach, I have their back.

Everything was settled: daily life and leisure time – up to that fateful day when my life would change entirely.

The company boss had asked me to interrupt my usual sales tour to meet with a very important, large client. This client had the highest priority, which meant I had to put another client on the back burner.

As I entered the client's sales room, my arms suddenly grew numb and I felt enormous pressure in my chest. I instinctively headed for the bathroom, but it was temporarily closed for cleaning. Then I called my wife who advised me to immediately ask the information desk to call a doctor. The desk was on the basement floor and I had already turned pale as a ghost! When I fell the floor in front of the bathroom, people just walked by without speaking to me or trying to help. They must have thought I was a homeless man who wanted to lie down.

In the interim my wife had alerted my boss on the phone. He drove immediately to the client to look after me. He was there in thirty minutes. In the meantime a few employees had assisted me, brought me to a nearby room and gave me something to drink. The lady at the information desk had called the paramedics who arrived within ten minutes. On their way to me, they had alerted the emergency doctor who arrived at nearly the same time as they did. In another ten minutes an ambulance with flashing lights took me to the nearest hospital. I was short of breath, full of anxiety and panic. In a word: I was scared to death.

My wife was called from the ambulance. She was wracked with worry. She worked in a preschool as a cook for hundreds of children. At first they didn't want to let her go because the children's food needed to be prepared. They finally let her go once she spoke with the head of the preschool about the seriousness of the situation.

The serious heart attack, the ensuing operation in which I received a stent and the fact that it was a matter of ten minutes that decided whether I lived or died raised my "new" life to an entirely new level of consciousness. The doctor later told me that if it had taken just a few minutes longer until I had received emergency medical care, my life would have been over because at that point the back wall of my heart was no longer receiving blood.

At the hospital I received quite a few visitors and I learned who was truly there for me in my life. My thirty-six year old boss offered me all the support I needed from the very beginning. I remembered then that one of my client's warehouse workers had had a heart attack just two weeks prior. He had died because he was home alone when it happened.

Life meant well by me. In the hospital I had enough time to reflect on the truly important things in life. Naturally I barely did any sports at all and my high blood pressure certainly didn't help, but at least I wasn't overweight.

I decided then and there in that hospital bed to turn my life around. After making good progress, I was released from the hospital for a three-week rehabilitation program. Despite the multiple daily treatments, I still had enough free time to think about my life's purpose, a question that was becoming more and more important as time went on.

How should my new life look?
What did I need to change?
What was truly important?
Was there really such a thing as a new beginning?
Who really had my back?
What was the point for my breakdown?

Six weeks after my heart attack, I went back to work. My boss said to me: Make a wish! And my wish was to work less and to care more for my key accounts. My boss was relieved that I was able to view my situation in this light and fulfilled my wish.

Shortly thereafter, I rescued a dog in Hungary who was about to be euthanized a week later. It was an opportunity to give this animal a new life out of sheer gratitude for my second chance.

What did I learn from all of this? Today I live much more mindfully, ride my bike often and go to the gym. I feel better, healthier, work less and enjoy my new life more.

My message is simple: The most important thing is self-care. Only then do we have enough energy to help others!

What chance would we have missed!

by Romy K.

When I was asked to write a story about a moment that changed my life I first thought about adventurous, dangerous or dramatic events in my life. On second thoughts though, I decided to write about a decision, which changed my life. A decision which I took because of the presence of inner strength, curiosity and most of all love. Therefore the following is dedicated to my brother B., without whom I wouldn't be who I am today.

At the age of 24 I was working full time as a Junior Sales Representative for a company which was nearly bankrupt. I was shifted in a city far away from home, family and friends and took care about an area, which I did not know any of the customers. Most of all my heart was broken and I had only one colleague who was sick of a slipped disk and did not come to work anymore. In a nutshell it was not the best time in my life.

I had to travel a lot and visit my customers in ''death of a salesman'' style and one evening in October I ended up in a hotel which looked and felt more like a health home than a warm and cozy place to spend the night. I was totally desperate, lonely and felt like choking. Standing on my room's balcony and looking at the dark northern sea I made the decision to quit my job and find inner peace again. The next day I did.

I applied for an internship in the company of my ex fellow students dad in Hong Kong, totally keen on a life time adventure. The job was mine and 4 months later I sat in the plane to Hong Kong. A new world opened up for me. I had a small room in the most Chinese area of Hong Kong, where I probably was the only European 24 year old girl. It was not at all the busy, shiny Hong Kong I expected. It was almost in mainland China and the taxi to central Hong Kong took me 50$. But I was happy.

After 3 months of my internship the boss of the company offered me a job as merchandise manager for an unlimited period of time. I was honored and happy but still it was a shock and it was not as if I could accept instantly. I know I had the most amazing time of my life in Hong Kong; I found friends, went out every evening, learned so much and finally had the life a young girl should have. Knowing if I want to live abroad in Hong Kong all by myself with a serious job and a responsibility was my task for the evening. I only had the night to make up my mind, the boss awaited my answer the next day.

My parents encouraged me later that evening on the phone to do the job on the one hand but on the other hand I felt my mother's sorrow to let her daughter go and live so far away from her. I hang up and sat on my bed crying, totally torn. The phone rang again.

It was my brother B., who is 16 years older than me who just said: '' I tell you one thing little sister, if you don't take this offer and you dare to come back to Germany declining that once in a lifetime offer I sit you back in the plane to Hong Kong straight away''. Boom! Here it was, he was absolutely right and he never doubted that I wouldn't be strong, smart and brave enough to take this job and live in China. Suddenly it was out of question and seemed as it was clear from the very beginning: of course I will stay in Hong Kong. The next day I went in my boss office and accepted his offer.

My new job title was Merchandise Manager and I was a supervisor of 19 colleagues for the coming two years ahead. With the worldwide financial crisis coming up in 2008 and the introduction of a new merchandise system in the company things changed. I worked 16hours a day, felt asleep every morning in the tube and suffered from a choleric boss. Retrospective I never experienced such a tough time in my working life but after that nothing did wow me anymore.

Times got better after a while and we recovered and went to daily routine. I became the personal assistant of my boss and finally came towards a normal work-life balance.

The next challenge was to find a new apartment by myself. Having the local Chinese newspaper in my hands I set out for a new flat. It was a Chinese experience. I came into houses where I was supposed to live with another family in 25qm, where there was no toilet or which were so full of shady people that the doorman needs to ask every entrant for their personal data. It was devastating and 35degrees in central Hong Kong, I only had one more flat to view and already given up hope. There it was, the most beautiful tiny place I had ever seen, but so full of lovely details that it was mine from the beginning on. I was lucky, and remember calling my mom and crying because I was giddy with pleasure.

The emotions I had had in Hong Kong were probably the shakiest and intense ones but they were totally worth it. It taught me that every emotion is important and that we need to deal with them otherwise they won't let us alone.

Living in Hong Kong was the biggest experience in my life and I am so thankful that my brother called that night. I never regretted it for one second. Sometimes you just need one person who uses the right words to catch you or rather pushes the right buttons to move you. My brother in that case believed in me and was so full of self-evident support and love that he would have gone mad if his little sister let this opportunity pass by. That was not the only time he helped me taking chances, which turned out right.

Some weeks ago I finally had the chance to help my brother with a decision, which hopefully starts to change his life. At the age of 49 my brother is unemployed, has a 7year old daughter to take care of and lives in my parents' house at the moment. He was very successful in very well-known advertising agencies for years but kind of never loved what he did and as consequence became tired and could not fulfill the demands of his industry anymore. He quit every job and started a new one and then realized that changing jobs is not the solution. Unemployed B. struggled to find out what he wants and lost time.

He was always fascinated with cars, garages and the smell of oil. The job of a car mechanic would have been something he always wanted to do, he told me. I felt it was my turn to intervene at this stage. I suggested that he should ask for an internship at a garage in the neighborhood, just to find out if it is really his dream and to have his foot in the door.

Three weeks ago B. started his experience as a car mechanic and he likes it. It is tougher than he expected but much more demanding for him than creating ad's. He made his first move towards a new future, same as I did in Hong Kong 8 years ago.

Finally it doesn't matter what we are doing to make a living or which choices we are taking. But what does matter is who is by our side.

Epilogue
by Ulrich Kellerer

Dear Readers,

We have come to the last story in this book. It is actually the reason the whole thing came to be! It was one further, deciding moment that turned my life upside down and brought about the most profound transformation.

In the summer of 2013 my mother fell down in her apartment and had to taken by ambulance to the hospital. When they called me, I made my way to the emergency room right away. Because I lived over forty miles away from my mother, it took me an hour before I could speak with the doctors.

The hospital professor explained to me that it was necessary to operate on her spine right away. He showed me where he needed to separate the bone from the vertebrae. Although it was hard for us laypeople to understand, we agreed to the operation. We would soon find out, however, that it was the wrong decision.

The surgery failed and my mother was paralyzed from the waist down! The doctors assured us that they would try further surgeries to repair the damage and do everything medically possible to regain my mother's mobility. I drove to the hospital every other day, sometimes by car and sometimes by train. Further surgeries followed, each time under general anesthesia. To add insult to injury, she got infected with a hospital germ that required we wear full-body protective clothing and masks during our visits to her.

After a total of seven failed surgeries, the doctors discovered that the support device around her spine that they had inserted to stabilize it at the beginning had gotten infected. They removed the frame, leaving a gapping hole in her back that just wouldn't heal.

Following her eighth surgery, I sought out the professor for a conversation. In response to my question if it was truly necessary to perform so many operations on an eighty-five year old, he claimed they were doing everything medically possible to alleviate my mother's pain. I suggested that perhaps it had more to do with the fact that she was at a university hospital in which every one of the young doctors should be granted an opportunity to "practice" and that might be why they performed so many operations. He did not respond to my comment.

She was then moved to a rehabilitation facility where she underwent two more surgeries to manage the pain. The rehabilitation did no good so we were forced to look for a good nursing home.

We were lucky! The most modern nursing home in Munich happened to be located directly across the street from my workplace. They even had an opening in a double room.

My mother agreed that the constant back and forth to the hospital had taken its toll on me. It was particularly advantageous that the nursing home was so close so I could visit her every day. In the beginning we even kept her apartment in the hopes that she could return there one day.

After a short time she pressed me to have her change to a single room because her roommate was exhausting. You normally have to wait up to two years for a single room so we had to get creative.

My mother needed "bonus points" so I firmly suggested to the nursing home management that I work there as a volunteer. Fully supported by my wife, I was asked to take over the service aspect of various parties in the home such as the spring festival, Carnival, the summer festival, "Oktoberfest" and Christmas. We served food and drinks to over two hundred residents and arranged the table decorations. We were also responsible for gathering those residents in wheelchairs so that they could partake in the festivities at the nursing home as well.

My mother didn't think much of my new position. "You are a manager and entrepreneur. You shouldn't be here serving coffee and cleaning up shattered glass!" she said with a frown.

My true intention in volunteering was a selfish one: I wanted to help my mother move into a single room as soon as possible. But I couldn't tell her that. I suggested to the nursing home management that I come once a week to read aloud to the residents for an hour. I loved it for two reasons: first, I absolutely adore reading and second, I had one distinct advantage with this particular audience. They were a captive audience as most of them weren't mobile ... Just kidding!

At any rate I could test out my performance abilities by seeing how my listeners responded and to see whether I was able to entertain people in a positive manner. It was my first step toward realizing a dream I have had all my life: to write books and do public speaking.

Management offered me Monday evenings at 7 p.m. It was after dinnertime at the nursing home. Reading aloud would be their final program point for the evening before they were brought to their rooms and to bed.

The first reading hour was a nightmare. How should I know how long an hour of reading could actually be? How in-depth should the story be to maintain the residents' attention without overwhelming them? Who would participate? How challenging could the book be?

My mother was rather skeptical and, of course, my biggest critic: "Speak louder! – Speak more clearly! – Pause every once in a while! – Take a sip of water!" She told me these things and much more. The other residents just stared at her because they didn't know at the time that she was my mother. Nonetheless, my ambition had been awakened. I improved my tone of voice, worked on my breathing techniques as well as my pronunciation.

My literature group met every Monday in the foyer café in basement of the nursing home. Week by week the number of listeners grew and my mother became more and more jealous. One time she snapped at me: "I'm not coming to your reading hour today because I've already taken a shower!" I didn't quite understand her argument, but it seemed she had already made her decision.

When my mother's condition worsened for which she required more intensive care, I shared with her the costs of the nursing home, the expense in keeping her apartment, etc. She told me I should look for a job rather than reading aloud at the nursing home.

Because of my family situation, I had vastly reduced the hours at my management job in the sales department of a well-known designer label. The company had appointed a young man to be my successor. My sabbatical was made possible thanks to my wife who owns the company with me. She also carries ninety percent of the sales for the women's collection so I was able to take a break to care for my mother.

I began visiting various seminars in the US as I worked toward my dream to write a book. The people around me didn't quite understand why I would give up such a successful career "just" to write. Furthermore, I was determined to give it a try in the most difficult and demanding market in the world and to write books in English and publish them in the US.

During one of the seminars, I met bestselling author Jack Canfield who suggested I write a series of books as he had done (*Chicken Soup for the Soul*). He gave me sound advice. As a result, my first book, *It's All About Fashion*, would appear shortly thereafter.

I spent my evenings doing webinars and teleseminars with the US. I was extremely motivated to live my "second" life. I felt unstoppable! I finally had a new project that my wife supported wholeheartedly. My mother was her typical skeptical self and didn't believe I would ever finish my book. For weeks on end I struggled with writer's block. At least ninety percent of my book was written on transatlantic flights to the US. I can't sleep on airplanes and I never wanted to watch a movie or the like. Instead, I took pen to paper and began to write.

Finally, after five months of sharing a room, my mother got the single room she had been looking for. At that point, she realized she wouldn't be returning to her own four walls and agreed to cancel the lease on her apartment. My wife and I handled the dismantling of her apartment, which was a bitter moment, knowing she would never see her home again.

The fact that she was paralyzed from the waist down and had to sit in a wheelchair wasn't as bad as having to spend her days with people suffering from dementia or other disabled people. It was "beneath her" and she struggled with that aspect of nursing home life. After just ten days in her own room, she fell again because she had wanted to go to the bathroom by herself. This time, she landed on the back of her head. She lay on the floor unconscious for some time before someone discovered her and took her to the hospital. Luckily, the X-rays didn't reveal any internal bleeding.

My mother was released from the hospital and allowed to return to the nursing home, but she was somehow rather defeated. On July 16, my deceased brother's birthday, I visited her for the last time. When we said good-bye, she told me: "I can't hold on any longer."

The following day at 7 a.m. my mother died in her bed. The nurse on duty called me. My wife and I said our good-byes, standing at her bedside with the pastor, caregivers and nurses. We lit a candle in her room and prayed for her.

My mother's passing marked yet another death in our family, leaving me as the last survivor of five.

It prompted me to think a lot about why I was the one to survive when every one else had departed. What was my purpose in this life?

The week of the funeral I understandably couldn't read aloud to the residents in the nursing home. The week after, however, I placed a picture of my mother on the podium and dedicated the reading hour to her.

The nursing home management was convinced that my "mission" had been accomplished: obtain a single room, mother deceased. There was no other reason to read aloud every week now ... or was there?

At this point, my transformation was already in full swing. It seemed impossible to me to let my reading group down. Some of them would even wait for me thirty minutes before it started. I had grown to love each and every one of the participants that I simply couldn't bear to abruptly stop it now. I would have mixed feelings as I entered the building every Monday evening. The daily glance over to my mother's old window still makes me sad to this day.

In November they held mass for all the deceased residents, lighting a candle for each of the deceased. I was shocked to see there had been fifty-one deceased residents in fifty-two weeks. That meant virtually one per week. I also noticed in the six months since I had started reading aloud how we had already lost four listeners. But a year later not a single one had died! It's a miracle.

The oldest listener is a lovely lady who is 107 years old!

In the interim our group has fixed seating arrangements and every one of us looks forward to this single hour every week. The women who come to the reading hour put on make-up and get gussied up for the occasion. We laugh a lot and everyone talks amongst themselves.

This one hour a week is a standing date for all of us. And on the rare occasion that I can't make it, I promise "my" old people to come the following Monday for sure.

It is hard to express in words what it means to me when a person pulls herself out her wheelchair to give me her hand and personally thank me for the reading hour. I have learned respect and humility from this place. With it I have gained a new perspective to appreciate life in all its forms.

This one hour a week has changed my life.

For thirty-six years I have tried to make people look good through fashion. Now I aim to do my best to make them *feel* good.

Each and every one of us can and should do all we can to be that which we truly are – human beings!

It is time to give back all that which we have received. It means a lot to me to motivate others and to make my contribution to ensure our co-existence on this Earth remains worth living.

Throughout my days I have learned that a single moment can change an entire life. And for those of you who have yet to experience it, you will. You will see.

With this in mind:
BECOME WHO YOU ALREADY ARE!

Acknowledgments

First of all deepest thanks to to my wife Inge. From the very first moment she supported me – not only in this book project – with help and advice and her infinite love.

Special thanks to my consultant and editor Silvia Kuttny-Walser. She is the soul of the project and managed in record time all necessary things to give this book shape and form and to help along the way to completion.

I am grateful to the team at Network! Agency. Thanks to Thilo Endemann for creating and hosting my website: www.ulrich-kellerer.com

Thanks a lot to my mentor Josef Schaaf. He was more than just friendly when he paved the way into the book world for me.

I thank my mentor in the US, Jack Canfield, who gave me the best recommendations and is always an inspiration for me.

Last but not least: Warmest thanks to the great people who put their trust in me and favored me with their personal stories, which made it possible to create this book the way it is.

Made in the USA
Columbia, SC
07 April 2018